London's Underworld

Anthem Travel Classics

Also in the series:

London: A *Pilgrimage* by Blanchard Jerrold and Gustav Doré
Persian Pictures by Gertrude Bell

London's Underworld

THOMAS HOLMES

with an Introduction by
Iain Sinclair

Anthem Press

Anthem Press
An imprint of Wimbledon Publishing Company
www.anthempress.com

This edition first published in UK and USA 2006
by ANTHEM PRESS
75-76 Blackfriars Road, London SE1 8HA, UK
or PO Box 9779, London SW19 7ZG, UK
and
244 Madison Ave. #116, New York, NY 10016, USA

First published in 1912

Introduction © Iain Sinclair 2006

British Library Cataloguing in Publication Data
A catalogue record for this book is available from the British Library.

Library of Congress Cataloging in Publication Data
A catalog record for this book has been requested.

1 3 5 7 9 10 8 6 4 2

ISBN 1 84331 219 0 (Pbk)

Illustrations courtesy of Dover Publications and the Museum of London.

Cover photograph: 'The Independent Shoe Black', from *Street Life in London*
by J Thompson and Adolphe Smith, 1887.

Printed in Malta

Contents

List of Illustrations

List of Illustrations

'Eyes that cannot Face the Light'

Thomas Holmes, with his tilted bowler, Wyatt Earp moustache, raised brows, belongs in the Old West: narrowed eyes burning out of a sepia album. A serious person capable of living on both sides of the law. A hard-bitten enforcer of morals. A bounty hunter for truth. Holmes, from what we know of him, his incessant prowling through London's subterranea, strove to be that most difficult thing, a good man in a bad place.

Settling in the suburbs, in Bedford Road, Tottenham, he respects a tradition established by upwardly-mobile police officers, fictional or documented. A short ride or a brisk stroll from the labyrinth, the ghetto, the criminous swamp. Alexander Baron's Inspector Merry from *King Dido* (1969)—a novel written in homage to Arthur Morrison—is a nice example of the type: courteous, dynamic, and on deceptively cosy terms with villains and malcontents. A recognised outsider, Merry enjoys the liberties of the shadow world, but returns, nightly, to his new home—which is to be found in 'an enclave of broad roads and classical villas in the midst of a poorer London.' In somewhere like De Beauvoir Town, on the Islington side of workaday Kingsland Road. Merry 'took a tram to Shoreditch and walked down Bethnal Green Road to the police station.' *King Dido* opens in 1911, the year before *London's Underworld* was published.

Thomas Holmes walks, walks, walks. Like Mayhew. Blanchard Jerrold. Thomas De Quincey. Like all the pilgrims, statisticians of poverty, reformers, visionaries fascinated by the machinery of the city, our ever-expanding metropolis. Holmes is always in movement, down among the vagrants and derelicts of the Embankment, steeling himself against the stench of some lodging-house kitchen (burnt sausages, smoke-fug, close-packed humanity). He misses nothing: clothes, hair, sallow skin, scuffed boots and bloodshot eyes. Prisons, charity pits, coffee stalls. He is a patron of London's invisibles; an undeceived listener to improbable and self-serving fictions. And, like all the other stalkers of the shallows, he is also a writer. Extinguished hopes, submerged districts, become the material of his direct and masculine prose. He will describe the horror, shame and degradation of lives endured at the limits of the possible. He will factor anecdotes, trade in the picaresque. The better to engage your attention, to pick your pocket (in a good cause). And he will find solutions. There is always, so Holmes believes, something to be done.

Having weighed the evidence, he reaches a firm conclusion. There is an echo here of his namesake, Sherlock. The villa in Tottenham becomes a version of the rooms of the consulting detective in Baker Street. There are constant interruptions of domestic quietude: beggars at the door, confidence men with impossible yarns, broken women. The sturdy Thomas Holmes, more Dr Watson than neurasthenic, cocaine-injecting detective, transcribes the stumbling biographies of human flotsam who float outside official history, the underclass of imperialism. Sad ghosts of those golden summers before the First War changed everything.

London's Underworld carries the dirt and misery of an earlier city; memory traces of Dickens, Gissing, of Jack London's *The People of the Abyss* (1903). But the abyss mapped by Holmes is more than a metaphor. Step out of line, suffer an industrial accident, a whim of fate, and you are gone: without status, dehumanised. Beyond the doubtful sanctuary of cheap rooms and cheaper furniture are the streets, doorways, parks. You fall and it is absolute. Holmes, prison reformer and secretary of the Howard Association, talks to the incarcerated, offers help to those he deems capable of helping themselves.

This was not the city of railways, electricity, orbital motorways imagined by Ford Madox Ford in *The Soul of London* (1905). Thomas Holmes, born in 1846 (when Dickens was labouring over *Dombey and*

Son in Switzerland), outlived Henry James by two years. But his prose is untainted by the ambiguities and self-doubts of Modernism. Freudian psychodramas, Jungian archetypes, the fractured perspectives of Vorticism, do not disturb a philosophy that is grounded in the particulars of locality. Holmes sees it as his business to challenge H.G. Wells, the Wells of *The Time Machine* (1895). 'Are we to have two distinct races! those above and those below? Is Wells' prophecy to come true; will one race become uncanny, loathsome abortions with clammy touch and eyes that cannot face the light?'

The pilgrimage into *London's Underworld* refutes Wellsian determinism: the city is stratified and divided, zones of light and clean air, zones of mephitic darkness, but the divisions can be healed. Holmes tells a plain, unembroidered tale, a report on which we are obliged to act. He cites: Ellen Langes, 59, a blouse-maker of Graham Road, Dalston, who starves to death. She is unable to get work and has sold all her household effects. The authorities show little interest in her case. She dies within sight of the German Hospital where Joseph Conrad was brought after his Congo collapse and where he meditated *The Heart of Darkness*. Not appreciating, perhaps, that it was here all along, within a few yards of his bed. The harsh consequences of shifts in market economics.

Rescued legends from the underworld are most often virtuoso displays of local colour, heroic tourism. The narrator descends from the civilised strata of society for a season and then returns with lurid episodes, sentimental cameos that are intended to shock. Jack London began his Whitechapel voyage, in the summer of 1902, by attending the offices of Thomas Cook. 'I went down into the under-world of London with an attitude of mind which I may best liken to that of an explorer.' He took his camera, he dressed in borrowed rags. He played a part. George Orwell (name changed, biography suppressed) followed the same path to the kitchens, skips and doss houses. He was fascinated and repelled by an exoticism of otherness. 'The room stank like a ferret's cage,' he wrote. 'You did not notice it when you got up, but if you went out and came back, the smell hit you in the face with a smack.'

There is no role-playing for Holmes. He makes himself known to his prey. He carries loose change. He describes what he sees. And describes it to a purpose: fresh ideas, change, action. Slums must be pulled down. Children freed from prisons. Charity wards will be properly managed. 'Some day when we are wise—but wisdom comes so slowly—these things will not be left to private enterprise, for municipalities will provide and own them at no loss to ratepayers either.'

When Holmes displays the gifts of a novelist, he is most engaging: he confesses his gullibility and promotes a kind of free-spirited vagrancy he knows must be lost. He can, at times, sound like a social engineer, a eugenicist—'I do not recommend a lethal chamber, but I do strongly advise permanent detention and segregation for those low types of unfortunate humanity'—but he speaks from what he has seen and never allows dogma to betray his quirky humanity.

This man with a passport to the lower depths meets Angus, an apparently blind seaman, who wanders the suburbs, 'looking for Bridlington on the road to Southgate.' Holmes knows he is being tricked, but he can't resist the lovely pitch. 'Its very audacity ensures success.' He stands at his Tottenham doorway, in dressing-gown and slippers, and offers charity to this ancient mariner with a story. And for that reason, for the spirit with which he pits himself against mock-piety and prejudice, we can forgive him anything. Even his reluctant assertion that all such wanderers should be removed from the public highway. We must, he concludes, establish 'special colonies for vagrants.' Holding camps, asylums. 'Every vagrant who could not give proof that he had some definite object in tramping must be committed to these colonies and detained, till such time as definite occupation or home can be found for him.' Such are the complexities, the problems for anyone proposing a solution to injustice, to the sickness and poverty Holmes discovered in his underworld. The villains and the wanderers of London are always present, moving at the edge of things, the limits of visibility. Men of large sympathy, drawn as much to write as to act, are their only witnesses. Their celebrants.

—Iain Sinclair

Preface

I am hopeful that some of the experiences given in the following chapters may throw a little light upon some curious but very serious social problems. Corporate humanity always has had, and always will have, serious problems to consider.

The more civilised we become the more complex and serious will be our problems—unless sensible and merciful yet thorough methods are adopted for dealing with the evils. I think that my pages will show that the methods now in use for coping with some of our great evils do not lessen, but considerably increase the evils they seek to cure.

With great diffidence I venture to point out what I conceive to be reasons for failure, and also to offer some suggestions that, if adopted, will, I believe, greatly minimise, if not remove, certain evils.

I make no claim to prophetic wisdom; I know no royal road to social salvation, nor of any specific to cure all human sorrow and smart.

But I have had a lengthened and unique experience. I have closely observed, and I have deeply pondered. I have seen, therefore I ask that the experiences narrated, the statements made, and the views expressed in this book may receive earnest consideration, not only from those who have the temerity to read it, but serious consideration also from our Statesmen and local authorities, from our Churches and philanthropists, from our men of business and from men of the world.

For truly we are all deeply concerned in the various matters which are dealt with in "London's Underworld."

Thomas Holmes
12, Bedford Road,
Tottenham, N.

I

My Friends
and Acquaintances

The odds and ends of humanity, so plentiful in London's great city, have for many years largely constituted my circle of friends and acquaintances.

They are strange people, for each of them is, or was, possessed of some dominating vice, passion, whim or weakness which made him incapable of fulfilling the ordinary duties of respectable citizenship.

They had all descended from the Upper World, to live out strange lives, or die early deaths in the mysterious but all pervading world below the line.

Some of them I saw, as it were, for a moment only; suddenly out of the darkness they burst upon me; suddenly the darkness again received them out of my sight.

But our acquaintance was of sufficient duration to allow me to acquire some knowledge, and to gain some experience of lives more than strange, and of characters far removed from the ordinary.

But with others I spent many hours, months, or years as circumstances warranted, or as opportunities permitted. Some of them became my intimates; and though seven long years have passed since I gave up police-court duties, our friendship bears the test of time, for they remain my friends and acquaintances still.

But some have passed away, and others are passing; one by one my list of friends grows less, and were it not that I, even now, pick up a new friend or two, I should run the risk of being a lonely old man. Let me confess, however, that my friends have brought me many worries, have caused me much disappointment, have often made me very angry. Sometimes, I must own, they have caused me real sorrow and occasionally feelings of utter despair. But I have had my compensations, we have had our happy times, we have even known our merry moments.

Though pathos has permeated all our intercourse, humour and comedy have never been far away; though sometimes tragedy has been in waiting.

But over one and all of my friends hung a great mystery, a mystery that always puzzled and sometimes paralysed me, a mystery that always set me to thinking.

Now many of my friends were decent and good-hearted fellows; yet they were outcasts. Others were intelligent, clever and even industrious, quite capable of holding their own with respectable men, still they were helpless.

Others were fastidiously honest in some things, yet they were persistent rogues who could not see the wrong or folly of dishonesty; many of them were clear-headed in ninety-nine directions, but in the hundredth they were muddled if not mentally blind.

Others had known and appreciated the comforts of refined life, yet they were happy and content amidst the horror and dirt of a common lodging-house! Why was it that these fellows failed, and were content to fail in life?

What is that little undiscovered something that determines their lives and drives them from respectable society?

What compensations do they get for all the suffering and privations they undergo? I don't know! I wish that I did! but these things I have never been able to discover.

Many times I have put the questions to myself; many times I have put the questions to my friends, who appear to know about as much and just as little upon the matter as myself.

They do not realise that in reality they do differ from ordinary citizens; I realise the difference, but can find no reason for it.

No! it is not drink, although a few of them were dipsomaniacs, for generally they were sober men.

I will own my ignorance, and say that I do not know what that little something is that makes a man into a criminal instead of constituting him into a hero. This I do know: that but for the possession of a little something, many of my friends, now homeless save when they are in prison, would be performing life's duties in settled and comfortable homes, and would be quite as estimable citizens as ordinary people.

Probably they would prove better citizens than the majority of people, for while they possess some inherent weakness, they also possess in a great degree many estimable qualities which are of little use in their present life.

These friends of mine not only visit my office and invade my home, but they turn up at all sorts of inconvenient times and places.—There is my friend the dipsomaniac, the pocket Hercules, the man of brain and iron constitution.

Year after year he holds on to his own strange course, neither poverty nor prison, delirium tremens nor physical injuries serve to alter him. He occupies a front seat at a men's meeting on Sunday afternoon when the bills announce my name. But he comes half drunk and in a talkative mood, sometimes in a contradictory mood, but generally good tempered. He punctuates my speech with a loud and emphatic "Hear! hear!" and often informs the audience that "what Mr. Holmes says is quite true!" The attendants cannot keep him silent, he tells them that he is my friend; he makes some claim to being my patron.

Poor fellow! I speak to him kindly, but incontinently give him the slip, for I retire by a back way, leaving him to argue my disappearance in no friendly spirit with the attendants. Yet I have spent many happy hours with him when, as sometimes happened, he was "in his right mind."

I, would like to dwell on the wonders of this man's strange and fearsome life, but I hasten on to tell of a contrast, for my friends present many contrasts.

4

I was hurrying down crowded Bishopsgate at lunch time, lost in thought, when I felt my hand grasped and a well-known voice say, "Why! Mr. Holmes, don't you know me?"

Know him! I should think I do know him; I am proud to know him, for I venerate him. He is only a French-polisher and by no means handsome, his face is furrowed and seamed by care and sorrow, his hands and clothing are stained with varnish. Truly he is not much to look at, but if any one wants an embodiment of pluck and devotion, of never-failing patience and magnificent love, in my friend you shall find it!

Born in the slums, he sold matches at seven years of age; at eight he was in an industrial school; his father was dead, his mother a drunkard; home he had none!

Leaving school at sixteen he became first a gardener's assistant, then a gentleman's servant; in this occupation he saved some money with which he apprenticed himself to french polishing. From apprentice to journeyman, from journeyman to business on his own account, were successive steps; he married, and that brought him among my many acquaintances.

He had a nice home, and two beautiful children, and then that great destroyer of home life, drink! had to be reckoned with. So he came to consult me. She was a beautiful and cultured woman and full of remorse.

The stained hands of the french polisher trembled as he signed a document by which he agreed to pay L1 per week for his wife's maintenance in an inebriate home for twelve months where she might have her babe with her. Bravely he did his part, and at the end of the year he brought her back to a new and better home, where the neighbours knew nothing of her past.

For twelve months there was joy in the home, and then a new life came into it; but with the babe came a relapse; the varnish-stained man was again at his wits' end. Once more she entered a home, for another year he worked and toiled to pay the charges, and again he provided a new home. And she came back to a house that he had bought for her in a new neighbourhood; they now lived close to me, and my house was open to them. The story of the following years cannot be told, for she almost ruined him. Night after night after putting the children to bed, he searched the streets and public-houses for her; sometimes I went with him. She pawned his clothes, the children's clothing, and even the boy's fiddle. He cleaned the house, he cooked the food, he cared for the children, he even washed and ironed their clothing on Saturday evening for the coming Sunday. He marked all the clothing, he warned all the pawnbrokers. At length he obtained a separation order, but tearing it up he again took her home with him. She went from bad to worse; even down to the deepest depths and thence to a rescue home. He fetched her out, and they disappeared from my neighbourhood.

So I lost them and often wondered what the end had been. To-day he was smiling; he had with him a youth of twenty, a scholarship boy, the violinist. He said, "I am just going to pay for his passage to Canada; he is going to be the pioneer, and perhaps we shall all join him, she will do better in a new country!" On further inquiry I found that she was trying hard, and doing better than when I lost them.

Thinking she needed greater interest in life, he had bought a small business for her, but "Mr. Holmes, she broke down!"

Alas! I knew what "breaking down" meant to the poor fellow, the heroic fellow I ought to have said. And so for her he will leave his kindred, home and friends; he will forsake the business that he has so slowly and laboriously built up, he will sacrifice anything in the hope that the air of Canada "will do her good." let us hope that it may, for her good is all he lives for, and her good is his religion.

Twenty years of heartbreaking misery have not killed his love or withered his hope. Surely love like his cannot fail of its reward. And maybe in the new world he will have the happiness that has been denied him in the old world, and in the evening of his life he may have the peaceful calm that has hitherto been denied him. For this he is seeking a place in the new world where the partner of his life and the desire of his eyes may not find it easy to yield to her besetting temptation, where the air and his steadfast love will "do her good."

But all my acquaintances are not heroes, for I am sorry to say that my old friend Downy has served his term of penal servitude, and is at liberty once more to beg or steal. He is not ashamed to beg, but I know that he prefers stealing, for he richly enjoys anything obtained "on the cross," and cares little for the fruits of honest labour.

Downy therefore never crosses my doorstep, and when I hold communication with him he stands on the doorstep where I bar his entrance.

Yet I like the vagabond, for he is a humorous rascal, and though I know that I ought to be severe with him, I fail dismally when I try to exhort him. "Now, look here, old man," he will say, "stop preaching; what are you going to do to help a fellow; do you think I live this life for fun" and his eyes twinkle! When I tell him that I am sure of it, he roars. Yes, I am certain of it, Downy is a thief for the fun of it; he is the worst and cleverest sneak I have the privilege of knowing; and yet there is such audacity about him and his actions that even his most reprehensible deeds do not disgust me.

He is of the spare and lean kind, but were he fatter he might well pose as a modern Jack Falstaff, for his one idea is summed up in Falstaff's words: "Where shall we take a purse to-night?" Downy, of course, obtained full remission of his sentence; he did all that was required of him in prison, and so reduced his five years' sentence by fifteen months. But I feel certain that he did nor spend three years and nine months in a convict establishment without robbing a good many, and the more difficult he found the task, the more he would enjoy it.

I expect his education is now complete, so I have to beware of Downy, for he would glory in the very thought of "besting" me, so I laugh and joke with the rascal, but keep him at arm's length. We discuss matters on the doorstep; if he looks ill I have pity on him, and subsidise him. Sometimes his merry look changes to a half-pathetic

7

look, and he goes away to his "doss house," realising that after all his "besting" he might have done better.

Some of my friends have crossed the river, but as I think of them they come back and bid me tell their stories. Here is my old friend the famous chess-player, whose books are the poetry of chess, but whose life was more than a tragedy. I need not say where I met him; his face was bruised and swollen, his jawbone was fractured, he was in trouble, so we became friends. He was a strange fellow, and though he visited my house many times, he would neither eat nor drink with us. He wore no overcoat even in the most bitter weather, he carried no umbrella, neither would he walk under one, though the rains descended and the floods came!

He was a fatalist pure and simple, and took whatever came to him in a thoroughly fatalist spirit. "My dear Holmes," he would say, "why do you break your heart about me? Let me alone, let us be friends; you are what you are because you can't help it; you can't be anything else even if you tried. I am what I am for the same reason. You get your happiness, I get mine. Do me a good turn when you can, but don't reason with me; let us enjoy each other's company and take things as they are."

I took him on his own terms; I saw much of him, and when he was in difficulties I helped him out.

For a time I became his keeper, and when he had chess engagements to fulfil I used to deliver him carriage paid to his destination wherever it might be. He always and most punctiliously repaid any monetary obligation I had conferred upon him, for in that respect I found him the soul of honour, poor though he was! As I think of him I see him dancing and yelling in the street, surrounded by a crowd of admiring East Enders, I see him bruised and torn hurried off to the police station, I see him standing before the magistrate awaiting judgment. What compensation dipsomania gave him I know not, but that he did get some kind of wild joy I am quite sure. For I see him feverish from one debauch, but equally feverish with the expectation of another.

With his wife it was another story, and I can see her now full of anxiety and dread, with no relief and no hope, except, dreadful as it may seem, his death! For then, to use her own expression, "she would know the worst." Poor fellow! the last time I saw him he was nearing the end. In an underground room I sat by his bedside, and a poor bed it was!

As he lay propped up by pillows he was working away at his beloved chess, writing chess notes, and solving and explaining problems for very miserable payments,

I knew the poverty of that underground room; and was made acquainted with the intense disappointment of both husband and wife when letters were received that did not contain the much-desired postal orders. And so passed a genius; but a dipsomaniac! A man of brilliant parts and a fellow of infinite jest, who never did justice to his great powers, but who crowded a continuous succession of tragedies into a short life. I am glad to think that I did my best for him, even though I failed. He has gone! but he still has a place in my affections and occupies a niche in the hall of my memory.

I very much doubt whether I am able to forget any one of the pieces of broken humanity that have companied with me. I do not want to forget them, for truth to tell they have been more interesting to me than merely respectable people, and infinitely more interesting than some good people.

But I am afraid that my tastes are bad, and my ideals low, for I am always happier among the very poor or the outcasts than I am with the decent and well behaved.

A fellow named Reid has been calling on me repeatedly; an Australian by birth, he outraged the law so often that he got a succession of sentences, some of them being lengthy. He tried South Africa with a like result; South Africa soon had enough of him, and after two sentences he was deported to England, where he looked me up.

He carries with him in a nice little case a certified and attested copy of all his convictions, more than twenty in number. He produces this without the least shame, almost with pride, and with the utmost confidence that it would prove a ready passport to my affection.

I talk to him; he tells me of his life, of Australia and South Africa; he almost hypnotises me, for he knows so much. We get on well together till he produces the "attested copy," and then the spell is broken, and the humour of it is too much for me, so I laugh.

He declares that he wants work, honest work, and he considers that his "certificate" vouches for his bona fides. This is undoubtedly true, but nevertheless I expect that it will be chiefly responsible for his free passage back to Australia after he has sampled the quality of English prisons.

My friends and acquaintances meet me or rather I meet them, in undesirable places; I never visit a prison without coming across one or more of them, and they embarrass me greatly.

A few Sundays ago I was addressing a large congregation of men in a London prison. As I stood before them I was dismayed to see right in the front rank an old and persistent acquaintance whom I thoroughly and absolutely disliked, and he knew it, for on more than one occasion I had good reason for expressing a decided opinion about him. A smile of gleeful but somewhat mischievous satisfaction spread over his face; he folded his arms across his breast, he looked up at me and quite held me with his glittering eye.

I realised his presence, I felt that his eye was upon me, I saw that he followed every word. He quite unnerved me till I stumbled and tripped. Then he smiled in his evil way.

I could not get rid of his eyes, and sometimes I half appealed to him with a pitiful look to take them off me. But it was no use, he still gazed at me and through me. So thinking of him and looking at him I grew more and more confused.

The clock fingers would not move fast enough for me. I had elected to speak on sympathy, brotherhood and mutual help. And this fellow to whom I had refused help again and again knew my feelings, and made the most of his opportunity.

But my friend will come and see me when he is once more out of prison. He will want to discuss my address of that particular Sunday afternoon. He will quote my words, he will remind me about sympathy and mutual help, he will hope to leave me rejoicing in the possession of a few shillings.

But that will be the hour of my triumph; for then I will rejoice in the contemplation of his disappointment as my door closes upon him. But if I understand him aright his personal failure will not lead him to despair, for he will appear again and again and sometimes by deputy, and he will put others as cunning as himself on my track.

Some time ago I was tormented with a succession of visitors of this description; my door was hardly free of one when another appeared. They all told the same tale: "they had been advised to come to me, for I was kind to men who had been in prison."

They got no practical kindness from me, but rather some wholesome advice. I found afterwards from a lodging-house habitué that this man had been taking his revenge by distributing written copies of my name and address to all the lodging-house inmates, and advising them to call on me. And I have not the slightest doubt that the rascal watched them come to my door, enjoyed their disappointment, and gloried in my irritation.

Yes, I have made the acquaintance of many undesirable fellows. and our introduction to each other has sometimes been brought about in a very strange manner. Sometimes they have forced themselves upon me and insisted upon my seeing much of them, and "knowing all about them" they would tell me of their struggles and endeavours to "go straight" and would put their difficulties and hopes before me. Specious clever rascals many of them were, far too clever for me, as I sometimes found out to my cost. One young fellow who has served a well-earned and richly merited sentence of five years' penal servitude, quite overpowered me with his good intentions and professions of rectitude. "No more prison for me," he would say; he brought his wife

11

and children to see me, feeling sure that they would form a passport to my sympathy and pocket.

He was not far wrong, for I substantially and regularly helped the wife. I had strong misgivings about the fellow, consequently what help I gave I took care went direct to his wife.

Sometimes he would call at my office, and with tears would thank me for the help given to his wife and children. I noticed a continual improvement in his clothing and appearance till he became quite a swell. I felt a bit uneasy, for I knew that he was not at work. I soon discovered, or rather the police discovered that he had stolen a lot of my office note-paper of which he had made free use, and when arrested on another charge several blank cheques which had been abstracted from my cheque book were found upon him. He had made himself so well known to and familiar with the caretaker of the chambers, that one night when he appeared with a bag of tools to put "Mr. Holmes' desk right," no questions were asked, and he coolly and quite deliberately, with the office door open, operated in his own sweet way. Fortunately, when trying the dodge in another set of chambers, he was arrested in the act, and my blank cheques among many others were found upon him.

Another term of penal servitude has stopped his career and put an end to, I will not say a friendship but an acquaintance, that I am not at any rate anxious to renew.

They come a long way to see me do some of my friends, and put themselves to some trouble in the matter, and not a little expense if they are to be believed. Why they do so I cannot imagine, for sometimes after a long and close questioning I fail to find any satisfactory reason for their doing so. I have listened to many strange stories, and have received not a few startling confessions! Some of my friends have gone comforted away when they had made a clean breast and circumstantially given me the details of some great crime or evil that they had committed. I never experienced any difficulty, or felt the least compunction in granting them plenary absolution; I never betrayed them to the police, for I knew that of the crime confessed they were as guiltless as myself. Of course there is a good deal of pathos about their actions, but I always felt a glow of pleasure when I could send poor deluded people away comforted; and I am sure that they really believed me when I told them that under no circumstances would I betray their confidence, or acquaint the police without first consulting them. I never had any difficulty in keeping my promise, though sometimes my friends would, after a long absence, remind me of it.

But occasionally one of my friends has compelled me to seek the advice of an astute detective, for very clever rogues, real and dangerous criminals, have been my companions and have boasted of my friendship, whilst pursuing a deplorably criminal course. But I never had the slightest compunction with regard to them when I knew beyond doubt what they were at. Friends and associates of criminals have more than once waited on me for the purpose of enlisting my sympathy and help for one of their colleagues who was about to be released from prison, and the vagabonds have actually informed detectives that "Mr. Holmes was going to take him in hand." What they really meant was, that they had taken Mr. Holmes in hand for the purpose of lulling the just suspicions of the police. One day not long ago a woman, expensively dressed and possessed of a whole mass of flaxen hair, burst into my office. She was very excited, spoke good English with an altogether exaggerated French accent, and her action was altogether grotesque and stereotyped. She informed me that she had that morning come from Paris to consult me. When I inquired what she knew about me and how she got my address, she said that a well-known journalist and a member of Parliament whom she had met in Paris had advised her to consult with me about the future of a man shortly to be discharged from prison. As during the whole of my life I had not met or corresponded with the brilliant gentleman she referred to, I felt doubtful, but kept silent. So on she went with her story, first, however, offering me a sum of money for the benefit of as consummate a villain as ever inhabited a prison cell.

I declined the money and refused to have anything to do with the matter till I had had further information. Briefly her story was as follows: The man in whom she and others were interested was serving a term of three years for burglary. He was an educated man, married, and father of two children. His wife loved him dearly, and his two children were "pretty, oh, so pretty!" They were afraid that his wife would receive him back again with open arms, and that other children might result. They were anxious that this should be prevented, for they felt, she was sorry to say, that he might again revert to crime, that other imprisonments might ensue, and that "the poor, poor little thing," meaning the wife, might be exposed to more and worse suffering than she had already undergone.

Would I receive a sum of money on his account and arrange for him to leave England? They felt that to be the wisest course, for "he is so clever, and can soon build up a home for her when he is away from his companions." Of his ability I had subsequently plenty of proof, and I have no reason to doubt her statement that he could soon "build up a home." He could very quickly—and a luxurious home, too!

The wife was not to be considered at all in the matter, but money would be sent to me from time to time to help the "poor little thing and her children!" I was interested, but I said to myself, "This is much too good," and the ready journey from Paris rather staggered me. I put a few simple questions, she pledged me to secrecy. I told her that I would ask the prison authorities to send him to me on his discharge.

"I so please, I now go back to Paris; I come again and I bring you money," she said, as she shook her furs and took herself and her flaxen hair to somewhere else than Paris, so I felt persuaded.

Two days before the prisoner's discharge she burst in again, huffy head, furs and gesticulation as before. "I come from Paris this morning, I bring you money." I was not present, but I had previously warned my assistant not to receive any money. The gay Parisian was informed that no money could be received, but she promptly put two sovereigns on the desk and disappeared—but not to Paris!

He stood before me at last, a little fellow, smart looking, erect, self-satisfied and self-reliant. I told him of the two sovereigns and the fluffy hair, of the good intentions of his Parisian friend. I spoke hopefully of a new life in a new country and of the future of his wife and children; he never blanched. He was quite sure he knew no French lady with fluffy hair; he had no friends, no accomplices; he wanted work, honest work; he intended to make amends for the past; he "would build up a home" for his wife and children.

I saw much of him; we lunched together and we smoked together, and he talked a good deal. His wife fell ill owing to very hard work, and I befriended her. He accepted the two pounds and asked for more! He was a citizen of the world, and spoke more than one language. Our companionship continued for some months, and then my friend and myself had to sever our connection.

He was one of a gang of very clever thieves, who operated on a large scale, and who for cool audacity and originality were, I think, almost unequalled!

They engaged expensive suites of rooms or flats, furnished them most expensively on credit or the hire system, insured the goods against burglary, promptly burgled themselves, sold the goods, realised the insurance, and then vanished to repeat their proceedings elsewhere.

So clever were they at the business that costly but portable goods were freely submitted to their tender mercies. They invariably engaged rooms that possessed a "skylight." It was my friend's business to do the burgling, and this he did by carefully removing the glass from the skylight, being careful not to break it; needless to say, he removed the glass from the inside and carefully deposited it on the roof, the valuables making their exit through the room door and down the staircase in broad daylight.

My friend, who spoke Dutch fluently and accurately, has, I understood, sold to English merchants whose probity was beyond dispute the proceeds of some of his "firm's" operations. This game went on for a time, the Parisian lady with the false hair being one of the confederates. He disappeared, however, and I am glad to think that for some considerable time society will be safeguarded from the woman with the flaxen hair, and the operations of a clever scoundrel.

I am glad to say that the number of my friends and acquaintances who have seriously tried to "best" me form but a small proportion of the whole. Generally they have, I believe, been animated with good intentions, though the failure to carry them out has frequently been manifest and deplorable.

I am persuaded that weakness is more disastrous to the world than absolute wickedness, for nothing in the whole of my life's experience has taken more out of me, and given me so much heartbreaking disappointment as my continued efforts on behalf of really well-intentioned individuals, who could not stand alone owing to their lack of grit and moral backbone. For redemptive purposes I would rather, a hundred times rather, have to deal with a big sinner than with a human jellyfish, a flabby man who does no great wrong, but on the other hand does not the slightest good.

But, as I have already said, though all my friends and acquaintances were dwellers in a dark land, not all of them were "known to the police"; indeed, many of them ought to be classified as "known to the angels," for their real goodness has again and again rebuked and inspired me.

Oh the patience, fortitude and real heroism I have met with in my acquaintances among the poor. Strength in time of trial, virtue amidst obscenity, suffering long drawn out and perpetual self-denial are characteristics that abound in many of my poorest friends, and in some of the chapters that are to follow I shall tell more fully of them, but just now I am amongst neither sinners nor saints, but with my friends "in motley." I mean the men and women who have occupied so much of my time and endeavours, but whose position I knew was hopeless.

How they interested me, those demented friends of mine! they were a perpetual wonder to me, and I am glad to remember that I never passed hard judgment upon them, or gave them hard words. And I owe much to them, a hundred times more than the whole of them are indebted to me; for I found that I could not take an interest in any one of them, nor make any fruitless, any perhaps foolish effort to truly help them, without doing myself more good than I could possibly have done to them. Fifteen years I stood by, and stood up for demented Jane Cakebread, and we became inseparably connected. She abused me right royally, and her power of invective was superb. When she was not in prison she haunted my house and annoyed my neighbours. She patronised me most graciously when she accepted a change of clothing from me; she lived in comparative luxury when I provided lodgings for her; she slept out of doors when I did not.

She bestowed her affections on me and made me heir to her non-existent fortune; she proposed marriage to me, although she frequently met and admired my good wife. All this and more, year after year!

Poor old Jane! I owe much to her, and I am quite willing, nay, anxious, to say that in a great measure Jane Cakebread was the making of Thomas Holmes.

Years have passed since we laid Jane gently to rest, but she comes back to me and dominates me whenever I mentally call my old friends together. Her voice is the loudest, her speech the most voluble, and her manner the most assertive of all my motley friends. They are all gathering around me as I write. My friend who teaches music by colour is here, my friend with his secret invention that will dispense with steam and electricity is here too; "Little Ebbs" the would-be policeman is here too; the prima donna whose life was more than a tragedy, the architect with his wonderful but never accepted designs, the broken artist with his pictures, the educated but non-sober lady who could convert plaster models into marble statuary are all with me. The unspeakably degraded parson smoking cigarettes, his absence of shirt hidden by a rusty cassock, lolls in my easy-chair; my burglar friend who had "done" forty years and was still asking for more, they are all around me! And my dipsomaniac friends have come too! I hear them talking and arguing, when a strident voice calls out, "No arguing! no arguing! argument spoils everything!" and Jane stops the talk of others by occupying the platform herself and recites a chapter from the book of Job. I am living it all over again!

And now troop in my suffering friends. Here is the paralysed woman of thirty-five who has for twenty years lain in bed the whiles her sister has worked incessantly to maintain her! Here is my widow friend who after working fifteen hours daily for years was dragged from the Lea. As she sits and listens her hands are making matchboxes and throwing them over her shoulder, one, two, three, four! right, left! they go to the imaginary heaps upon the imaginary beds. While blighted children are crawling upon the floor looking up at me with big eyes. Here is my patient old friend who makes "white flowers" although she is eighty years of age, and still keeps at it, though, thank God, she gets the old-age pension.

Now come in the young men and maidens, the blighted blossoms of humanity who wither and die before the time of fruition, for that fell disease consumption has laid its deadly hand upon them.

Oh! the mystery of it all, the sorrow and madness of it all! I open my door and they file out. Some back to the unseen world, some back to the lower depths of this world! Surely they are a motley lot, are my friends and acquaintances; they are as varied as humanity itself. So they represent to me all the moods and tenses of humanity, all its personal, social and industrial problems. I have a pitiful heart; I try to keep a philosophic mind; I am cheery with them; I am doubtful, I am hopeful!

I never give help feeling sure that I have done wisely, I never refuse the worst and feel sure that I have done well. I live near the heart of humanity, I count its heart-beats, I hear its throbs.

I realise some of the difficulties that beset us, I see some of the heights and depths to which humanity can ascend or descend. I have learned that the greatest factors in life are kindly sympathy, brotherly love, a willingness to believe the best of the worst, and to have an infinite faith in the ultimate triumph of good!

II

London's Underworld

London's great underworld to many may be an undiscovered country. To me it is almost as familiar as my own fireside; twenty-five years of my life have been spent amongst its inhabitants, and their lives and circumstances have been my deep concern.

Sad and weary many of those years have been, but always full of absorbing interest. Yet I have found much that gave me pleasure, and it is no exaggeration when I say that some of my happiest hours have been spent among the poorest inhabitants of the great underworld.

But whether happy or sorrowful, I was always interested, for the strange contrasts and the ever-varying characteristics and lives of the inhabitants always compelled attention, interest and thought. There is much in this underworld to terrorise, but there is also much to inspire.

Horrible speech and strange tongues are heard in it, accents of sorrow and bursts of angry sound prevail in it.

Drunkenness, debauchery, crime and ignorance are never absent; and in it men and women grown old in sin and crime spend their last evil days. The whining voice of the professional mendicant is ever heard in its streets, for its poverty-stricken inhabitants readily respond to every appeal for help.

So it is full of contrasts; for everlasting toil goes on, and the hum of industry ever resounds. Magnificent self-reliance is continually exhibited, and self-denial of no mean order is the rule.

The prattle of little children and the voice of maternal love make sweet music in its doleful streets, and glorious devotion dignifies and illumines the poorest homes.

But out of the purlieus of this netherworld strange beings issue when the shades of evening fall.

Men whose hands are against every man come forth to deeds of crime, like beasts to seek their prey! Women, fearsome creatures, whose steps lead down to hell, to seek their male companions.

Let us stand and watch!

Here comes a poor, smitten, wretched old man; see how he hugs the rags of his respectability; his old frayed frock-coat is buttoned tightly around him, and his outstretched hands tell that he is eager for the least boon that pity can bestow. He has found that the way of the transgressor is hard; he has kissed the bloom of pleasure's painted lips, he has found them pale as death!

But others follow, and hurry by. And a motley lot they are; figure and speech, complexion and dress all combine to create dismay; but they have all one common characteristic. They want money! and are not particular about the means of getting it. Now issue forth an innumerable band who during the day have been sleeping off the effects of last night's debauch. With eager steps, droughty throats and keen desire they seek the wine cup yet again.

Now come fellows, young and middle-aged, who dare not be seen by day, for whom the police hold "warrants," for they have absconded from wives and children, leaving them chargeable to the parish.

Here are men who have robbed their employers, here young people of both sexes who have drained Circe's cup and broken their parents' hearts.

Surely it is a strange and heterogeneous procession that issues evening by evening from the caves and dens of London's underworld. But notice there is also a returning procession! For as the sun sinks to rest, sad-faced men seek some cover where they may lie down and rest their weary bones; where perchance they may sleep and regain some degree of passive courage that will enable them, at the first streak of morning light, to rise and begin again a disheartening round of tramp, tramp, searching for work that is everlastingly denied them. Hungry and footsore, their souls fainting within them, they seek the homes where wives and children await their return with patient but hopeless resignation.

Take notice if you will of the places they enter, for surely the beautiful word "home" is desecrated if applied to most of their habitations. Horrid places within and without, back to back and face to face they stand.

At their doorway death stands ready to strike. In the murky light of little rooms filled with thick air child-life has struggled into existence; up and down their narrow stairs patient endurance and passive hopelessness ever pass and repass.

Small wonder that the filthy waters of a neighbouring canal woo and receive so many broken hearts and emaciated bodies.

But the procession now changes its sex, for weary widowed women are returning to children who for many hours have been lacking a mother's care, for mothers in the underworld must work if children must eat.

So the weary widows have been at the wash-tubs all day long, and are coming home with two shillings hardly earned. They call in at the dirty general shop, where margarine, cheese, bread, tinned meat and firewood are closely commingled in the dank air.

A loaf, a pennyworth of margarine, a pennyworth of tea, a bundle of firewood, half a pound of sugar, a pint of lamp-oil exhaust their list of purchases, for the major part of their earnings is required for the rent.

So they climb their stairs, they feed the children, put them unwashed to bed, do some necessary household work, and then settle down themselves in some shape, without change of attire, that they may rest and be ready for the duties of the ensuing day. Perhaps sweet oblivion will come even to them. "Blessings on the man who invented sleep," cried Sancho Panza, and there is a world of truth in his ecstatic exclamation, "it wraps him round like a garment."

Aye, that it does, for what would the poor weary women and men of London's underworld do without it? What would the sick and suffering be without it? In tiny rooms where darkness is made visible by penny-worths of oil burned in cheap and nasty lamps, there is no lack of pain and suffering, and no lack of patient endurance and passive heroism.

As night closes in and semi-darkness reigns around, when the streets are comparatively silent, when children's voices are no longer heard, come with me and explore!

It is one o'clock a.m., and we go down six steps into what is face-tiously termed a "breakfast parlour"; here we find a man and woman about sixty years of age. The woman is seated at a small table on which stands a small, evil-smelling lamp, and the man is seated at another small table, but gets no assistance from the lamp; he works in comparative gloom, for he is almost blind; he works by touch.

For fifty years they have been makers of artificial flowers; both are clever artists, and the shops of the West End have fairly blazed with the glory of their roses. Winsome lassie's and serene ladies have made themselves gay with their flowers.

There they sit, as they have sat together for thirty years. Neither can read or write, but what can be done in flowers they can do. Long hours and dark rooms have made the man almost blind.

He suffers also from heart disease and dropsy. He cannot do much, but he can sit, and sit, while his wife works and works, for in the underworld married women must work if dying husbands are to be cared for.

So for fifteen hours daily and nightly they sit at their roses! Then they lie down on the bed we see in the corner, but sleep does not come, for asthma troubles him, and he must be attended and nursed.

Shall we pay another visit to that underworld room? Come, then. Two months have passed away, the evil-smelling lamp is still burning, the woman still sits at the table, but no rose-leaves are before her; she is making black tulips. On the bed lies a still form with limbs decently smoothed and composed; the poor blind eyes are closed for ever. He is awaiting the day of burial, and day after day the partner of his life and death is sitting, and working, for in this underworld bereaved wives must work if husbands are to be decently buried. The black tulips she will wear as mourning for him; she will accompany his poor body to the cemetery, and then return to live alone and to finish her work alone.

But let us continue our midnight explorations, heedless of the men and women now returning from their nightly prowl who jostle us as they pass.

We enter another room where the air is thick and makes us sick and faint. We stand at the entrance and look around; we see again the evil-smelling lamp, and again a woman at work at a small table, and she too is a widow!

She is making cardboard boxes, and pretty things they are. Two beds are in the room, and one contains three, and the other two children. On the beds lie scores of dainty boxes. The outside parts lie on one bed, and the insides on the other. They are drying while the children sleep; by and by they will be put together, tied in dozens, and next morning taken to the factory. But of their future history we dare not inquire.

The widow speaks to us, but her hands never rest; we notice the celerity of her movements, the dreadful automatic certainty of her touch is almost maddening; we wait and watch, but all in vain, for some false movement that shall tell us she is a human and not a machine. But no, over her shoulder to the bed on the left side, or over her shoulder to the bed on her right side, the boxes fly, and minute by minute and hour by hour the boxes will continue to grow till her task is completed. Then she will put them together, tie them in dozens, and lay herself down on that bed that contains the two children.

Need we continue? I think not, but it may give wings to imagination when I say that in London's underworld there are at least 50,000 women whose earnings do not exceed three halfpence per hour, and who live under conditions similar to those described. Working, working, day and night, when they have work to do, practically starving when work is scarce.

The people of the underworld are not squeamish, they talk freely, and as a matter of course about life and death. Their children are at an early age made acquainted with both mysteries; a dead child and one newly born sometimes occupy a room with other children.

People tell me of the idleness of the underworld and there is plenty of it; but what astonishes me is the wonderful, the persistent, but almost unrewarded toil that is unceasingly going on, in which even infants share.

Come again with me in the day-time, climb with me six dark and greasy flights of stairs, for the underworld folk are sometimes located near the sky.

In this Bastille the passages are very narrow, and our shoulders sometimes rub the slimy moisture from the walls. On every landing in the semi-darkness we perceive galleries running to right and to left. On the little balconies, one on every floor, children born in this Bastille are gasping for air through iron bars.

There are three hundred suites of box rooms in this Bastille, which means that three hundred families live like ants in it. Let us enter No. 250. Time: 3.30 p.m. Here lives a blind matchbox-maker and his wife with their seven children. The father has gone to take seven gross of boxes to the factory, for the mother cannot easily climb up and down the stone stairs of the Bastille. So she sits everlastingly at the boxes, the beds are covered with them, the floor is covered with them, and the air is thick with unpleasant moisture.

One, two, three, four, there they go over her shoulder to the bed or floor; on the other side of the table sits a child of four, who, with all the apathy of an adult if not with equal celerity, gums or pastes the labels for his mother. The work must be "got in," and the child has been kept at home to take his share in the family toil.

In this Bastille the children of the underworld live and die, for death reaps here his richest harvest. Never mind! the funeral of one child is only a pageant for others. Here women work and starve, and here childhood, glorious childhood, is withered and stricken; but here, too, the wicked, the vile, the outcast and the thief find sanctuary.

The strange mixture of it all bewilders me, fascinates me, horrifies me, and yet sometimes it encourages me and almost inspires me. For I see that suffering humanity possesses in no mean degree those three great qualities, patience, fortitude and endurance.

For perchance these three qualities will feel and grope for a brighter life and bring about a better day.

Though in all conscience funerals are numerous enough in this bit of the underworld, and though the conditions are bad enough to destroy its inhabitants, yet the people live on and on, for even death itself sometimes seems reluctant to befriend them.

Surely there is nothing in the underworld so extraordinary as the defiance flung in the face of death by its poor, feeble, ill-nourished, suffering humanity.

According to every well-known rule they ought to die, and not to linger upon the order of their dying. But linger they do, and in their lingering exhibit qualities which ought to regenerate the whole race. It is wonderful upon what a small amount of nourishment humanity can exist, and still more wonderful under what conditions it can survive.

Shall we look in at a house that I know only too well? Come again, then!

Here sits an aged widow of sixty-four at work on infants' shoes, a daughter about twenty-six is at work on infants' socks. Another daughter two years older is lying on her back in an invalid's chair, and her deft fingers are busily working, for although paralysis has taken legs, the upper part of her body has been spared. The three live together and pool their earnings; they occupy two very small rooms, for which they pay five shillings weekly.

After paying twopence each to avoid parish funerals, they have five shillings left weekly for food, firing, clothing and charity. Question them, and you will learn how they expend those five shillings. "How much butter do you allow yourselves during the week?" The widow answers: "Two ounces of shilling butter once a week." "Yes, mother," says the invalid, "on a Saturday." She knew the day of the week and the hour too, when her eyes brightened at the sight of three-halfpenny worth of butter. Truly they fared sumptuously on the Sabbath, for they tasted "shilling butter."

But they refuse to die, and I have not yet discovered the point at which life ebbs out for lack of food, for when underworld folk die of starvation we are comforted by the assurance that they died "from natural causes."

I suppose that if the four children all over eight years of age, belonging to a widow machinist well known to me, had died, their death would have been attributed to "natural causes." She had dined them upon one pennyworth of stewed tapioca without either sugar or milk. Sometimes the children had returned to school without even that insult to their craving stomachs. But "natural causes" is the euphonious name given by intelligent juries to starvation, when inquests are held in the underworld. Herein is a mystery: in the land of plenty, whose granaries, depots, warehouses are full to repletion, and whose countless ships are traversing every ocean, bringing the food and fruits of the earth to its shores, starvation is held to be a natural cause of death.

Here let me say, and at once, that the two widows referred to are but specimens of a very large company, and that from among my own acquaintances I can with a very short notice assemble one thousand women whose lives are as pitiful, whose food is as limited, whose burdens are as heavy, but whose hearts are as brave as those I have mentioned.

The more I know of these women and their circumstances, the more and still more I am amazed. How they manage to live at all is a puzzle, but they do live, and hang on to life like grim death itself. I believe I should long for death were I placed under similar conditions to those my underworld friends sustain without much complaining.

They have, of course, some interests in life, especially when the children are young, but for themselves they are largely content to be, to do, and to suffer.

Very simple and very limited are their ambitions; they are expressed in the wish that their children may rise somehow or other from the world below to the world above, where food is more plentiful and labour more remunerative. But my admiration and love for the honest workers below the line are leading me to forget the inhabitants that are far removed from honesty, and to whom industry is a meaningless word.

There are many of them, and a mixed lot they are. The deformed, the crippled and the half-witted abound. Rogues and rascals, brutes in human form, and human forms that are harking back to the brute abound also. With some we may sound the lowest depths, with others we may ascend to glorious heights. This is the wonder of underworld. Some of its inhabitants have come down, and are going lower still. Others are struggling with slippery feet to ascend the inclined plane that leads to the world above. Some in their misery are feebly hoping for a hand that will restore them to the world they have for ever lost!

And there are others who find their joy in this netherworld! For here every restraint may be abandoned and every decency may be outraged. Here are men and women whose presence casts a blight upon everything fresh and virtuous that comes near them.

Here the children grow old before their time, for like little cubs they lie huddled upon each other when the time for sleep comes. Not for them the pretty cot, the sweet pillow and clean sheets! but the small close room, the bed or nest on the floor, the dirty walls and the thick air. Born into it, breathing it as soon as their little lungs begin to operate, thick, dirty air dominates their existence or terminates their lives.

"Glorious childhood" has no place here, to sweet girlhood it is fatal, and brave boyhood stands but little chance.

Though here and there one and another rise superior to environment and conditions, the great mass are robbed of the full stature of their bodies, of their health, their brain power and their moral life.

But their loss is not the nation's gain, for the nation loses too! For the nation erects huge buildings falsely called workhouses, tremendous institutions called prisons. Asylums in ever-increasing numbers are required to restrain their feeble bodies, and still feebler minds!

Let us look at the contrasts! Their houses are so miserably supplied with household goods that even a rash and optimistic man would hesitate before offering a sovereign for an entire home, yet pawnshops flourish exceedingly, although the people possess nothing worth pawning. Children are half fed, for the earnings of parents are too meagre to allow a sufficient quantity of nourishing food; but public-houses do a roaring trade on the ready-money principle, while the chandler supplies scraps of food and half-ounces of tea on very long credit.

Money, too, is scarce, very scarce, yet harpies grow rich by lending the inhabitants small sums from a shilling up to a pound at a rate of interest that would stagger and paralyse the commercial world. Doctors must needs to content with a miserable remuneration for their skilled and devoted services, when paid at all! but burial societies accumulate millions from a weekly collection of ill-spared coppers. Strangest of all, undertakers thrive exceedingly, but the butcher and baker find it hard work to live.

Yes, the underworld of London is full of strange anomalies and queer contradictions. When I survey it I become a victim to strange and conflicting emotions.

Sometimes I am disgusted with the dirt and helplessness of the people. Sometimes I burn with indignation at their wrongs. But when I enter their houses I feel that I would like to be an incendiary on a wholesale scale. Look again! I found the boot-machinist widow that I have mentioned, in Bethnal Green; she was ill in bed, lying in a small room; ill though she was, and miniature as the room was, two girls aged twelve and fourteen slept with her and shared her bed, while a youth and a boy slept in a coal-hole beneath the stairs. Nourishment and rest somewhat restored the woman, and to give her and the

29

children a chance I took for them a larger house. I sent them bedding and furniture, the house being repaired and repainted, for the previous tenant had allowed it to take fire, but the fire had not been successful enough! I called on the family at midday, and as I stood in the room, bugs dropped from the ceiling upon me. The widow's work was covered with them; night and day the pests worried the family, there was no escaping them; I had to fly, and again remove the family. How can the poor be clean and self-respecting under such conditions!

For be it known this is the normal condition of thousands of human habitations in London's great underworld. How can cleanliness and self-respect survive? Yet sometimes they do survive, but at a terrible cost, for more and still more of the weekly income must go in rent, which means less and still less for food and clothing. Sometimes the grossness and impurity, the ignorance and downright wickedness of the underworld appal and frighten me.

But over this I must draw a veil, for I dare not give particulars; I think, and think, and ask myself again and again what is to be the end of it all! Are we to have two distinct races! those below and those above? Is Wells' prophecy to come true; will the one race become uncanny, loathsome abortions with clammy touch and eyes that cannot face the light? Will the other become pretty human butterflies? I hope not, nay, I am sure that Wells is wrong! For there is too much real goodness in the upper world and too much heroism and endurance in the underworld to permit such an evolution to come about.

But it is high time that such a possibility was seriously considered. It is high time, too, that the lives and necessities, the wrongs and the rights of even the gross poor in the underworld were considered.

For the whole social and industrial system is against them. Though many of them are parasites, preying upon society or upon each other, yet even they become themselves the prey of other parasites, who drain their blood night and day.

So I ask in all seriousness, is it not high time that the exploitation of the poor, because they are poor, should cease. See how it operates: a decent married woman loses her husband; his death leaves her dependent upon her own labour. She has children who hitherto have been provided with home life, food and clothing; in fact the family had lived a little above the poverty line, though not far removed from it.

She had lived in the upper world, but because her husband dies, she is precipitated into the lower world, to seek a new home and some occupation whereby she and her children may live.

Because she is a widow, and poor and helpless, she becomes the prey of the sweater. Henceforth she must work interminable hours for a starvation wage. Because she is a mother, poor and helpless, she becomes the prey of the house farmer. Henceforward half her earnings must go in rent, though her house and its concomitants are detestable beyond words.

But though she is poor, her children must be fed, and though she is a widowed mother, she, even she, must eat sometimes. Henceforward she must buy food of a poor quality, in minute quantities, of doubtful weight, at the highest price. She is afraid that death may enter her home and find her unprepared for a funeral, so she pays one penny weekly for each of her children and twopence for herself to some collection society.

All through this procedure her very extremities provide opportunities to others for spoliation, and so her continued life in the underworld is assured. But her children are ill-nourished, ill-clothed, ill-lodged and ill-bathed, and the gutter is their playground. They do not develop properly in mind or body, when of age they are very poor assets considered financially or industrially. They become permanent residents of the underworld and produce after their kind.

So the underworld is kept populated from many sources. Widows with their children are promptly kicked into it, others descend into it by a slow process of social and industrial gravitation. Some descend by

31

the downward path of moral delinquency, and some leap into it as if to commit moral and social death.

And surely 'tis a mad world! How can it be otherwise with all this varied and perplexed humanity seething it, with all these social and industrial wrongs operating upon it. But I see the dawn of a brighter day! when helpless widow mothers will no longer be the spoil of the sweater and the house "farmer." The dawn has broke! before these words are printed thousands of toiling women in London's underworld will rejoice! for the wages of cardboard box-makers will be doubled. The sun is rising! for one by one all the terrible industries in which the women of the underworld are engaged will of a certainty come within the operations of a law that will stay the hand of the oppressors. And there will be less toil for the widows and more food for the children in the days that are to be.

But before that day fully comes, let me implore the women of the upper world to be just if not generous to the women below. Let me ask them not to exact all their labours, nor to allow the extremities of their sisters to be a reason for under-payment when useful service is rendered. Again I say, and I say it with respect and sorrow, that many women are thoughtless if not unjust in their business dealings with other women.

I am more concerned for the industrial and social rights of women than I am for their political rights; votes they may have if you please. But by all that is merciful let us give them justice! For the oppression of women, whether by women or men, means a perpetuation of the underworld with all its sorrows and horrors; and the under-payment of women has a curse that smites us all the way round.

And if a word of mine can reach the toiling sisters in the netherworld, I would say to them: Be hopeful! Patient I know you to be! enduring you certainly are! brave beyond expression I have found you. Now add to your virtues, hope!

For you have need of it, and you have cause for it. I rejoice that so many of you are personally known to me! You and I, my sisters, have had much communion, and many happy times together; for sometimes we have had surcease from toil and a breath of God's fresh air together.

Be hopeful! endure a little longer; for a new spirit walks this old world to bless it, and to right your long-continued wrongs.

Oh! how you have suffered, sisters mine! and while I have been writing this chapter you have all been around me. But you are the salt of the underworld; you are much better than the ten just men that were not found in Sodom. And when for the underworld the day of redemption arrives, it will be you, my sisters, the simple, the suffering, enduring women that will have hastened it!

So I dwell upon the good that is in the netherworld, in the sure and certain hope, whether my feeble words and life help forward the time or not, that the day is not far distant when the dead shall rise! When justice, light and sweetness will prevail, and in prevailing will purify the unexplored depths of the sad underworld.

I offer no apology for inserting the following selections from London County Council proceedings. Neither do I make any comment, other than to say that the statements made present matters in a much too favourable light.

"LONDON'S CHILD SLAVES
"OVERWORK AND BAD NUTRITION
"Disclosures in L.C.C. Report.
(From the Daily Press, December 1911)

"The comments passed by members of the L.C.C. at the Education Committee meeting upon the annual report of the medical officer of that committee made it clear that many very interesting contents of the report had not been made public.

"The actual report, which we have now seen, contains much more that deserves the serious attention of all who are interested in the problem of the London school child.

"There is, for example, a moving page on child life in a north-west poverty area, where, among other conditions, it is not uncommon to find girls of ten doing a hard day's work outside their school work; they are the slaves of their mothers and grandmothers.

"The great amount of anaemia and malnutrition among the children in this area (says the report) is due to poverty, with its resultant evils of dirt, ill-feeding and under-feeding, neglect and female labour.

"Cheap food.—The necessity for buying cheap food results in the purchasing of foodstuffs which are deficient in nutrient properties. The main articles of diet are indifferent bread and butter, the fag ends of coarse meat, the outside leaves of green vegetables, and tea, and an occasional pennyworth of fried fish and potatoes. Children who are supplied with milk at school, or who are given breakfast and dinner, respond at once to the better feeding, and show distinct improvement in their class work. The unemployment among the men obliges the women to seek for work outside the home, and the under-payment of female labour has its effect upon the nutrition of the family.

"'Investigation in the senior departments of one school showed that 144 children were being supported by their mothers only, 57 were living on their sisters, 68 upon the joint earnings of elder brothers and sisters, while another 130 had mothers who went out to work in order to supplement the earnings of the father.

"'Approximately one-third of the children in this neighbourhood are supported by female labour. With the mother at work the children rapidly become neglected, the boys get out of control, they play truant, they learn to sleep out, and become known to the police while they are still in the junior mixed department.'

"The Girl Housewife.—The maintenance of the home, the cooking and catering, is done by an elderly girl who sometimes may not be more than ten years of age. The mother's earnings provide bread and tea for the family and pay the rent, but leave nothing over for clothing or boots.

"Many of the boys obtain employment out of school hours, for which they are paid and for which they may receive food; others learn to hang about the gasworks and similar places, and get scraps of food and halfpence from the workmen. In consequence they may appear to be better nourished than the girls 'who work beyond their strength at domestic work, step cleaning, baby minding, or carrying laundry bundles and running errands.' For this labour they receive no remuneration, since it is done for the family.

"A remarkable paragraph of the report roundly declares—

" 'The provision generally at cost price of school meals for all who choose to pay for them would be a national economy, which would do much to improve the status of the feeding centres and the standard of feeding. This principle is applied most successfully in schools of a higher grade, and might well be considered in connection with the ordinary elementary schools of the Council. Such a provision would probably be of the greatest benefit to the respectable but very poor, who are too proud to apply for charity meals, and whose children are often penalised by want, and the various avoidable defects or ailments that come in its train.'

"Feeding wanted.—Of the children of a Bethnal Green school, the school doctor is quoted as reporting that 'it was not hospital treatment but feeding that was wanted.'

"Among curious oddments of information contained in the report, it is mentioned that the children of widows generally show superior physique.

"The teeth are often better in children from the poorer homes, 'perhaps from use on rougher food materials which leaves less DEBRIS to undergo fermentation.'

" 'Children of poorer homes also often have the advantage of the fresh air of the streets, whilst the better-off child is kept indoors and becomes flabby and less resistant to minor ailments. The statistics of infantile mortality suggest that the children of the poorer schools have also gone through a more severe selection; disease weeding out by natural selection, and the less fit having succumbed before school age, the residue are of sturdier type than in schools or classes where such selection has been less intense.'"

III

The Nomads

A considerable portion of the inhabitants of the world below the line are wanderers, without home, property, work or any visible means of existence. For twenty years it has been the fashion to speak of them as the "submerged," and a notable philanthropist taught the public to believe that they formed one-tenth of our population.

It was currently reported in the Press that the philanthropist I have referred to offered to take over and salve this mass of human wreckage for the sum of one million pounds. His offer was liberally responded to; whether he received the million or not does not matter, for he has at any rate been able to call to his assistance thousands of men and women, and to set them to work in his own peculiar way to save the "submerged."

From a not unfriendly book just published, written by one who was for more than twenty years intimately associated with him, and one of the chief directors of his salvage work, we learn that the result has largely been a failure.

To some of us this failure had been apparent for many years, and though we hoped much from the movement, we could not close our eyes to facts, and reluctantly had to admit that the number of the "submerged" did not appreciably lessen.

True, shelters, depots, bridges, homes and labour homes were opened with astonishing celerity. Wood was chopped and paper sorted in immense quantities, but shipwrecked humanity passed over bridges that did not lead to any promised land, and abject humanity ascended with the elevators that promptly lowered them to depths on the other side.

Stimulated by the apparent success or popularity of the Salvation Army, the Church Army sprang into existence, and disputed with the former the claim to public patronage, and the right to save! It adopted similar means, it is certain with similar results, for the "submerged" are still with us.

I say that both these organisations pursued the same methods and worked practically on the same lines, for both called into their service a number of enthusiastic young persons, clothed them in uniforms, horribly underpaid them, and set them to work to save humanity and solve social and industrial problems, problems for which wiser and more experienced people fail to find a solution. It would be interesting to discover what has become of the tens of thousands of enthusiastic men and women who have borne the uniform of these organisations for periods longer or shorter, and who have disappeared from the ranks.

How many of them are "submerged" I cannot say, but I know that some have been perilously near it.

I am persuaded that this is a dangerous procedure, very dangerous procedure, and the subscribing public has some right to ask what has become of all the "officers" who, drawn from useful work to these organisations, have disappeared.

But as a continual recruiting keeps up the strength, the subscribing public does not care to ask, for the public is quite willing to part with its vested interests in human wreckage. All this leads me to say once more that the "submerged" are still with us. Do you doubt it? Then come with me; let us take a midnight walk on the Thames Embankment; any night will do, wet or dry, winter or summer!

Big Ben is striking the hour as we commence our walk at Blackfriars; we have with us a sack of food and a number of second-hand overcoats. The night is cold, gusty and wet, and we think of our warm and comfortable beds and almost relinquish our expedition. The lights on Blackfriars Bridge reveal the murky waters beneath, and we see that the tide is running out.

We pass in succession huge buildings devoted to commerce, education, religion and law; we pass beautiful gardens, and quickly we arrive at the Temple. The lamps along the roadway give sufficient light for our purpose, for they enable us to see that here and there on the seats and in the recesses of the Embankment are strange beings of both sexes.

Yonder are two men, unkempt and unshaven, their heads bent forward and their hands thrust deep into their trousers pockets and, to all appearance, asleep.

Standing in a sheltered corner of the Temple Station we see several other men, who are smoking short pipes which they replenish from time to time with bits of cigars and cigarettes that they have gathered during the day from the streets of London.

I know something of the comedy and tragedy of cigar ends, for times and again I have seen a race and almost a struggle for a "fat end" when some thriving merchant has thrown one into the street or gutter. Suddenly emerging from obscurity and showing unexpected activity, two half-naked fellows have made for it; I have seen the satisfaction of the fellow who secured it, and I have heard the curse of the disappointed; but there! at any time, on any day, near the Bank, or the Mansion House, in Threadneedle Street, or in Cheapside such sights may be seen by those who have eyes to see.

These two fellows have been successful, for they are assuaging the pangs of hunger by smoking their odds and ends. They look at us as we pass to continue our investigation. Here on a seat we find several men of motley appearance; one is old and bent, his white beard covers his chest, he has a massive head, he is a picturesque figure, and would stand well for a representation of Old Father Thames, for the wet streams from his hair, his beard and his ample moustache. Beside him sits a younger man, weak and ill. His worn clothing tells us of better days, and we instinctively realise that not much longer will he sit out the midnight hours on the cold Embankment.

Before we distribute our clothes and food, we continue our observation. What strikes us most is the silence, for no one speaks to us, no hand is held out for a gift, no requests are made for help.

They look at us unconcernedly as we pass; they appear to bear their privations with indifference or philosophy. Yonder is a woman leaning over the parapet looking into the mud and water below; we speak to her, and she turns about and faces us. Then we realise that Hood's poem comes into our mind; we offer her a ticket for a "shelter," which she declines; we offer her food, but she will have none of it; she asks us to leave her, and we pass on.

Here is a family group, father and mother with two children; their attire and appearance tell us that they are tramps; the mother has a babe close to her breast, and round it she has wrapt her old shawl; a boy of five sits next to her, and the father is close up.

The parents evidently have been bred in vagrancy, and the children, and, unless the law intervenes, their children are destined to continue the species. The whining voice of the woman and the outstretched hands of the boy let us know that they are eager and ready for any gift that pity can bestow.

But we give nothing, and let me say that after years of experience, I absolutely harden my heart and close my pocket against the tramping beggar that exploits little children. And to those who drag children, droning out hymns through our quiet streets on Sunday, my sympathies extend to a horsewhip.

We leave the tramps, and come upon a poor shivering wretch of about thirty-five years; his face presents unmistakable signs of disease more loathsome than leprosy; he is not fit to live, he is not fit to die; he is an outcast from friends, kindred and home. He carries his desolation with him, and the infirmary or the river will be the end of him.

Here are two stalwart fellows, big enough and strong enough to do useful work in the world. But they are fresh from prison, and will be back in prison before long; they know us, for it is not the first time we have made their acquaintance.

They are by no means backward in speaking and telling us that they want "just ten shillings to buy stock in Houndsditch which they can sell in Cheapside." As we move away they beg insistently for "just a few shillings; they don't want to get back to prison."

Now we come to a youth of eighteen; he seems afraid, and looks at us with suspicious eyes; what is he doing here? We are interested in him, so young, yet alone on the Embankment. We open our bag and offer him food, which he accepts and eats; as we watch him our pity increases: he is thinly clad, and the night air is damp and cold; we select an old coat, which he puts on. Then we question him, and he tells us that his mother is dead, his father remarried; that his stepmother did not like him, and in consequence his father turned him out; that he cannot get work. And so on; a common story, no originality about it, and not much truth!

We suddenly put the question, "How long have you lived in lodging-houses?" "About three years, sir." "What did you work at?" "Selling papers in the streets." "Anything else?" "No, sir." "You had not got any lodging money to-night.?" "No." "Ever been in prison?" "Only twice." "What for?" "Gambling in the streets," and we leave him, conscious that he is neither industrious, honest nor truthful.

We come at length to Waterloo Bridge, and here in the corners and recesses of the steps we find still more of the submerged, and a pitiful lot they are.

We look closely at them, and we see that some are getting back to primeval life, and that some are little more than human vegetables. We know that their chief requirements are food, sleep and open air; and that given these their lives are ideal, to themselves! But we distribute our food amongst them, we part with our last old coat, we give tickets for free shelters, but we get no thanks, and we know well enough that the shelter tickets will not be used, for it is much easier for philosophic vagabondage to remain curled up where it is than to struggle on to a shelter.

So we leave them, and with a feeling of hopelessness hurry home to our beds.

But let us revisit the Embankment by day at 11 a.m. We take our stand right close to Cleopatra's Needle; we see that numbers of wretched people, male and female, are already there, and are forming themselves into a queue three deep, the males taking the Westminster side of the Needle, the females the City side.

While this regiment of a very dolorous army is gathering together, and forming silently and passively into the long queue, we look at the ancient obelisk, and our mind is carried backward to the days of old, when the old stone stood in the pride of its early life, and with its clear-cut hieroglyphics spoke to the wonderful people who comprised the great nation of antiquity.

We almost appeal to it, and feel that we would like to question it, as it stands pointing heavenwards beside our great river. Surely the ancient stone has seen some strange sights, and heard strange sounds in days gone by.

Involuntarily we ask whether it has seen stranger sights, and heard more doleful sounds than the sights to be seen under its shadow to-day, and the sounds to be heard around it by night. Could it speak, doubtless it would tell of the misery, suffering, slavery endured by the poor in Egypt thousands of years ago. Maybe it would tell us that the great empire of old had the same difficulties to face and the same problems to solve that Great Britain is called upon to face and to solve to-day.

For the poor cried for bread in the days of the Pharaohs, and they were crowded into unclean places, but even then great and gorgeous palaces were built.

"Can you tell us, Ancient Stone, has there been an onward march of good since that day? Are we much better, wiser, happier and stronger than the dusky generations that have passed away?" But we get no response from the ancient stone, as grim and silent it stands looking down upon us. So we turn to the assembled crowd. See how it has grown whilst we have been speculating. Silently, ceaselessly over the various bridges, or through the various streets leading from the Strand they have come, and are still coming.

There is no firm footstep heard amongst them as they shufflingly take their places. No eager expectation is seen on any face, but quietly, indifferently, without crushing, elbowing, they join the tail-end of the procession and stand silently waiting for the signal that tells them to move.

Let us walk up and down to count them, for it is nearly twelve o'clock, and at twelve o'clock the slow march begins. So we count them by threes, and find five hundred men to the right and one hundred women to the left, all waiting, silently waiting! Stalwart policemen are there to keep order, but their services are not required.

In the distance the whirl of London's traffic raises its mighty voice; nearer still, the passing tramcars thunder along, and the silence of the waiting crowd is made more apparent by these contrasts.

Big Ben booms the hour! it is twelve o'clock! and the slow march begins; three by three they slowly approach the Needle, and each one is promptly served with a small roll of bread and a cup of soup; as each one receives the bread and soup he steps out of the ranks, promptly and silently drinks his soup, and returns the cup. Rank follows rank till every one is served, then silently and mysteriously the crowd melts away and disappears. The police go to other duties, the soup barrows are removed; the grim ancient stone stands once more alone.

But a few hours later, even as Big Ben is booming six, the "Miserables" will be again waiting, silently waiting for the rolls of bread and the cups of soup, and having received them will again mysteriously disappear, to go through the same routine at twelve o'clock on the morrow. Aye! and to return on every morrow when soup and rolls are to be had.

It looks very pitiful, this mass of misery. It seems very comforting to know that they are fed twice a day with rolls and soup, but after all the matter wants looking at very carefully, and certain questions must be asked.

Who are these miserables? How comes it that they are so ready to receive as a matter of course the doles of food provided for them?

Are they really helped, and is their position really improved by this kind of charity? I venture to say no! I go farther, and I say very decidedly that so long as the bulk of these people can get food twice a day, and secure some kind of shelter at night, they will remain content to be as they are. I will go still farther and say, that if this provision becomes permanent the number of the miserables will increase, and the Old Needle will continue to look down on an ever-growing volume of poverty and wretchedness.

For after receiving the soup and bread, these nomads disappear into the streets and by-ways of London, there by hook or crook, by begging or other means, to secure a few coppers, to pick up scraps of food, and to return to the Embankment.

I have walked up and down the Embankment, I have looked searchingly at the people assembled. Some of them I have recognised as old acquaintances; many of them, I know, have no desire to be other than what they are. To eat, to sleep, to have no responsibility, to be free to live an uncontrolled life, are their ambitions; they have no other. Some of them are young men, only twenty years of age, who have seen the inside of prison again and again. Some of them are older, who have tramped the country in the summer time and have been drawn to London by the attraction of an easy feeding in the winter. Search their ranks! and you will find very little genuine, unfortunate, self-respecting poverty. They are what they are, and unless other means are adopted they will, remain what they are!

And so they will eat the bread and drink the soup; they will come at twelve o'clock noon; they will come at six o'clock in the evening. They will sleep where they can, and to-morrow will be as to-day; and the next day as to-morrow, unless some compulsion is applied to them.

All this is very sad, but I venture to say it is true, and it seems to be one of the evils almost inseparable from our present life. Probably in every clime and every age such women and men have existed. The savage lives in all of us, and the simple life has its attractions.

To be free of responsibility is, no doubt, a natural aspiration. But when I see how easy it is for this class of people to obtain food, when I see how easy it is for them to obtain shelter, when I see and know how thousands of the poor are unceasingly at work in order to provide a modicum of food and the semblance of a shelter, then it occurs to me, and I am sure it will to any one who thinks seriously upon the matter, that these men and women, who are harking back to the life of the idle savage, are treated better in Christian England than the industrious, self-respecting but unfortunate poor. But come with me to see another sight! It is again afternoon, and we take our stand at 3.30 p.m. outside a shelter for women which every night receives, for fourpence each, some hundreds of submerged women.

The doors will not be opened till six o'clock, so we are in time to watch them as they arrive to take their places in the waiting queue. A policeman is present to preserve order and keep the pavement clear; but his service is not required, for the women are very orderly, and allow plenty of room for passers-by.

As the time for opening approaches, the number of waiting women increases until there is a waiting silent crowd. No photograph could give the slightest idea of their appearance, for dirt and misery are not revealed by photography.

Let us look at them, for the human eye sees most! What do we see? Squalor, vice, misery, dementia, feeble minds and feeble bodies. Old women on the verge of the grave eating scraps of food gathered from the City dustbins. Dirty and repulsive food, dirty and repulsive women! who have begged during the day enough coppers to pay for their lodging by night. Girls of twenty, whose conduct in their homes has been outrageous, and whose life in London must be left to imagination. Middle-aged women, outcasts, whose day has past, but who have still capabilities for begging and stealing. The whole company presents an altogether terrible picture, and we are conscious that few of the women have either the ability or the desire to render decent service to the community, or to live womanly lives.

At length the door opens, and we watch them pass silently in, to sleep during the night in the boxes arranged on the floors, their bodies unwashed, and their clothing unchanged. Happy are such women when some trumpery theft lands them in prison, for there at any rate a change of clothing is provided, and a bath is compulsory.

If we stand outside a men's shelter, we see a similar state of things, a waiting crowd. A passive, content, strange mixed lot of humans. Some of them who have been well educated, but are now reaping the harvest that follows the sowing of wild oats. The submerged males are, on the whole, less repulsive than the women; dirt is less in evidence, and they exhibit a better standard of health. But many of them are harking back to nature, and remind us of the pictures we have seen of primeval man.

I want to say a few words about the submerged that congregate on the Thames Embankment, and the humanity we have seen enter the cheap shelters.

My experience has shown me that they constitute the lowest grade and the least hopeful class of the submerged. Amongst them there are very few decent and helpable men and women who are capable of rising to a higher life. Say what we will, be as pitiful as we may, those of us who have much experience of life know perfectly well that there exists a large class of persons who are utterly incapable of fulfilling the duties of decent citizenship. It may be that they are wicked, and it is certain that they are weak, but whether wicked or weak, they have descended by the law of moral gravitation and have found their level in the lowest depths of civilised life.

And they come from unexpected quarters, for some who have known comfort and refinement are now quite content with their present conditions. Whether born of refined parents, or of rude and ignorant parents, whether coming from a tramping stock, or from settled home life, they have one thing in common. It is this—the life they live has a powerful attraction for them; they could not if they would, and would not if they could, live lives that demand decency, discipline and industry.

47

Nothing but compulsion will ever induce them to submit themselves to disciplined life. But let it be clearly understood that I am now speaking only of the lowest class of the submerged. While my experience has taught me that they, humanly speaking, are a hopeless lot, I have learned that they have their qualities. They can endure if they cannot work; they can suffer if they cannot strive. After all I am persuaded that they get a fair amount of happiness. Simple pleasures are the greatest, perhaps the only real pleasures. We all like to be free of responsibilities. There is no rent-day coming round with dread certainty and irritating monotony to the nomads. No rate collector irritates them with his imperious "demand note." No school-board officer rouses them to a sense of duty by his everlasting efforts to force their children to school. No butcher, no baker, no milkman duns them for payment of bills long overdue! They escape the danger of furniture on the "hire system." For them no automatic gas meter grudgingly doles out its niggardly pennyworths of gas. They are not implored to burden themselves with the ENCYCLOPAEDIA BRITANNICA.

They are free from the seductions of standard bread; paper-bag cookery causes them no anxious thought. Even "sweet peas" do not enter into their simple calculations. Finally no life assurance agent marks them for his prey, and no income-tax tempts them to lie! From all these things they are free, and I would like to know who would not wish to be free of them and a thousand other worries I would escape them if I could, but alas I cannot.

Decidedly there is much to be said for the life of a nomad, but whether or not I should place him among the inhabitants of the underworld I am not sure; for he toils not, neither does he spin, and his bitterest enemies cannot accuse him of taking thought for the morrow. I had almost forgotten one great advantage he possesses: he need not wash; and when this distasteful operation becomes, for sanitary reasons, absolutely necessary, why then he can take a month in one of our great sanatoria, either prison or workhouse will do, and be thoroughly cleansed!

The idea of such free and easy folk being saved by a shelter and wood-chopping is very funny.

But we are all tramps, more or less; it is only a question of degree! Who would not like to tramp with George Borrow through Spain or Wales I would like the chance! Who does not feel and hear the "call of the wild"? Most certainly all Britons thrill with it. Who does not like to feel the "wind on the heath" beat on his face and fill his nostrils! Who does not love the sweetness of country lanes, or the solitude of mountains, or the whispering mystery of the wood, or the terrors of the sea, or the silence of midnight?

All these things are ingrained in us, part and parcel of our very selves; we cannot get away from them if we would, and woe betide us if we did! For this is a grand quality in itself, one that has made our nation and our empire. But couple it with idleness, inertia, feebleness, weak minds, and weaker bodies; why, then you get the complete article, the vegetable human! the guinea-pig man; if you will, the "submerged," or at any rate a portion of them.

Originally I have no doubt the human family were nomads, and many of our good old instincts still survive, but civilisation has killed others. In every cross-bred species of animals or plants there are "reverts" or "throwbacks," and the human family produces plenty of them. Every civilised country has its "throwbacks," and the more monotonous civilisation becomes, the more cast-iron its rules, and the more scientific and educated its people, the more onerous and difficult become the responsibilities and duties of citizenship; and the greater the likelihood of in increased number of reverts to undisciplined and wild life. In this direction the sea and our colonies are the safeguard of England. But to-day we pay in meal or malt for our civilisation, for many brave lads, with thews and muscles, are chafing, fretting and wearing out their hearts in dull London offices or stores, where they feel choked, hampered, cabined and confined, for civilisation chains them to their desks.

But I am wandering too! I will hark back. Another cause, and a fruitful cause, of nomadic life is to be found in the ever-increasing number of young incapables that our present-day life produces. Characterless, backboneless, negative kind of fellows with neither wisdom nor stature abound. Up to eighteen years they pass muster, but after that age they are useless; in reality they need caring for all their lives. They possess no initiative, no self-reliance, and little capability for honest work, unless it be simple work done under close supervision. Our industrial life is too strenuous for these young men; they are laggards in life's race, they quickly fall behind, and ultimately become disqualified altogether.

Many of their parents refuse them shelter, the streets become their home; absolute idleness supervenes; their day is past. Henceforward they are lodging-house habitués, or wanderers on the face of the earth.

More pitiable still is the case of those that may be classed as feeble-minded, and who are just responsible enough to be quite irresponsible. Idiots and imbeciles have largely disappeared from country villages and small towns. They are well taken care of, for our large asylums are full of them; they have good quarters, good food, every attention, so they live long in the land.

But the case is very different with the half imbeciles or the half mad. Short terms of imprisonment with short periods of hopeless, useless liberty and an occasional spell in the workhouse constitute the circle of their lives; and a vicious circle it is. Can any life be more pitiable? Sane enough to know that they are not quite sane, insane enough to have no wish to control their animal or vicious instincts. Possessing no education, strength or skill, of no possible use in industrial life, with no taste for decency or social life; sleeping by day in our parks, and by night upon the Embankment. But they mate; and as like meets with like the result may be imagined! Here again we are paying for our neglect of many serious matters. Bad housing, overcrowding, incessant work by the mothers whilst bearing children, drinking habits among the parents, insufficient food for the children, endless anxieties and worries. All these things and more amongst that portion of the nation which produces the largest families; what wonder that many incapable bodies and minds result!

But if civilisation allows all this, civilisation must pay the penalty, which is not a light one, and continue to have the miserables upon the Embankment.

Have we no pity! no thought for the next generation, no concern for ourselves! No! I do not recommend a lethal chamber, but I do strongly advise permanent detention and segregation for these low types of unfortunate humanity. Nothing less will avail, and expensive though it might be for a time, it would pay in the near future, and would be at once an act of mercy and justice.

Yes, on the Thames Embankment extremes meet, the ages are bridged over, for the products of our up-to-date civilisation stand side by side with the products of primeval habits and nomadic life.

IV

Lodging-Houses

The inmates of the underworld lodging-houses are a queer and heterogeneous lot; but they are much to be preferred to the sleepers out; because rascally though many of them are, there is a good deal of self-reliance and not a little enterprise amongst them. By hook and crook, and, it is to be feared, mostly by crook, they obtain sufficient money for food and lodging, and to this extent they are an improvement upon the sleepers out. They have, too, some pluck, perseverance and talents that, rightly applied, might be of considerable benefit to the community. But having got habituated to the liberty of common lodging-houses, and to the excitement of getting day by day just enough for each day's need, though sometimes fasting and sometimes feasting, the desire for settled home life and for the duties of citizenship has vanished. For with the money to pay night by night for their lodgings, responsibility to rent and tax collector ends.

I must allow some exceptions, for once every year there comes upon thousands of them the burden of finding five shillings to pay for the hawker's licence that provides them with the semblance of a living, or an excuse for begging. After much experience of this class, including many visits to common lodging-houses, and some friendships with the inmates, I am sure that the desire to be untrammelled with social and municipal obligation leads a great percentage of the occupants to prefer the life to any other. They represent to some extent in this modern and industrial age the descendants of Jonadab, the son of Rechab, with this exception, they are by no means averse to the wine-cup. It is to be feared that there is a growth in this portion of our community, for every scheme for providing decent lodgings for casually homeless men is eagerly taken advantage of by men who might and who ought to live in homes of their own, and so fulfil the duties of decent citizenship. In this respect even Lord Rowton's estimable lodging-houses, and those, too, of our municipal authorities prove no exception, for they attract numbers of men who ought not to be there, but who might, with just a little more self-reliance and self-respect, live comfortably outside.

But I pass on to the common lodging-houses that accommodate a lower class than is found in municipal or Rowton houses. Probably none, or at any rate very few, of my readers have had a practical experience of common lodging-houses. I have, so therefore I ask them to accompany me to one of them.

In a dingy slum stand a number of grimy houses that have been converted into one big house. The various doorways have been blocked and one enlarged entrance serves.

As we enter, the money-taker in his office demands our business. We tell him that we are anxious to have a look round, and he tells us that he will send for the deputy. The deputy is the autocrat that governs with undisputable sway in this domain of semi-darkness and dirt. We stand aside in the half-lit passage, taking good care that we have no contact with the walls; the air we breathe is thick with unpleasant odours, and we realise at once, and to our complete satisfaction, the smell and flavour of a common lodging-house. We know instinctively that we have made its acquaintance before, it seems familiar to us, but we are puzzled about it until we remember we have had a foretaste of it given to us by some lodging-house habitués that we met. The aroma of a common lodging-house cannot be concealed, it is not to be mistaken. The hour is six o'clock p.m., the days are short, for it is November. The lodgers are arriving, so we stand and watch them as they pass the little office and pay their sixpences. Down goes the money, promptly a numbered ticket takes its place; few words are exchanged, and away go the ticket-holders to the general kitchen.

Presently the deputy comes to interview us, and he does not put us at our ease; he is a forbidding fellow, one that evidently will stand no nonsense. Observe, if you please, that he has lost his right hand, and that a formidable iron hook replaces it. Many a time has that hook been serviceable; if it could speak, many tales would it tell of victories won, of rows quelled, and of blood spilled.

We have seen the fellow previously, and more than once, at the local police-court. Sometimes he came as prosecutor, sometimes as prisoner, and at other times as witness. When the police had been required to supplement the power of his iron hand in quelling the many free fights, he appeared sometimes in the dual capacity of prisoner and prosecutor.

We know that he retains his position because of his strength and the unscrupulous way in which he uses it. He knows us too, but he is not well pleased to see us! Nevertheless, he accedes to our request for "just a look round." So through a large passage we pass, and he ushers us into the lodging-house kitchen. As the door opens a babel of many voices greets us, a rush of warm air comes at us, and the evidence of our noses proclaims that bloaters and bacon, liver and onions, sausages and fresh fish are being cooked. We look and see, we see and taste! Strange eyes are turned upon us just for a moment, but we are not "'tecs," so the eyes are turned back to the different frying-pans or roasting-forks, as the case may be. See how they crowd round the huge and open fire, for there is no cooking range. See how they elbow each other as they want space for this pan or that fork. See how the bloaters curl and twist as if trying to escape from the forks and the fire. See how the sausages burst and splutter in their different pans. See how stolidly the tough steaks brown, refusing either to splutter, yield fat, or find gravy to assist in their own undoing.

Listen to the sizzling that pervades the place, acting as an orchestral accompaniment to the chorus of human voices. Listen to it all, breathe it all, let your noses and your ears take it all in. Then let your eyes and your imagination have their turn before the pungency of rank tobacco adds to the difficulty of seeing and breathing. And so we look, and we find there are sixty human beings of both sexes and various ages in that kitchen. Some of them we know, for have we not seen them in Cheapside, St. Paul's Churchyard, or elsewhere acting as gutter merchants. Yonder sit an old couple that we have seen selling matches or laces for many years past! It is not a race day, and there being no "test match" or exciting football match, a youth of sixteen who earns a precarious living by selling papers in the streets sits beside them. To-day papers are at a discount, so he has given up business for the day and sought warmth and company in his favourite lodging-house.

Ah! there is our old friend, the street ventriloquist! You see the back of his hand is painted in vivid colours to resemble the face of an old woman. We know that he has a bundle that contains caps and bonnets, dresses and skirts that will convert his hand and arm into a quaint human figure. Many a droll story can he tell, for he has "padded the hoof" from one end of England to the other; he knows every lodging-house from Newcastle-on-Tyne to Plymouth. He is a graceless dog, fond of a joke, a laugh and a story; he is honest enough and intelligent enough for anything. But of regular life, discipline and work he will have none. By and by, after the cooking is all done, he will want to give a performance and take up a collection.

There are a couple, male and female, who tramp the country lanes; the farm haystacks or outbuildings have been their resting-places during the summer, but approaching winter has sent them back to London.

You see that they have got a tattered copy of Moody and Sankey's hymns, which is their stock-in-trade. They have at different lodging-house "services" picked up some slight knowledge of a limited number of tunes, now they are trying to commit the words to memory.

To-morrow they will in quiet streets be whining out "Oh, where is my boy to-night?" or "Will you meet me at the Fountain?"

Look again—here is a shabby-genteel man who lives by his wits. He is fairly educated and can write a plausible letter. He is dangerous; his stock-in-trade comprises local directories, WHO'S WHO, annual reports of charitable societies, clergymen's lists, etc. He is a begging-letter writer, and moves from lodging-house to lodging-house; he writes letters for any of the inmates who have some particular tale of woe to unfold, or some urgent appeal to make, and he receives the major part of the resultant charity.

He is drunken and bestial, he is a parasite of the worst description, for he preys alike on the benevolent and upon the poor wretches whose cause he espouses.

He assumes many names, he changes his addresses adroitly, and ticks off very carefully the names and addresses of people he has defrauded. In fact, he is so clever and slippery that the police and the Charity Organisation Society cannot locate him. So he thrives, a type of many, for every one of London's common lodging-houses can provide us with one or more such cunning rogues.

Yonder sits a "wandering boy" about twenty-eight years of age. He is not thriving, and he must needs be content with simple bread and cheese. A roll of cheap "pirated" music lies on his knee and proclaims his method of living. His life has its dangers, for he has great difficulty in providing five shillings for his pedlar's licence, and he runs great risk of having his stock seized by the police, and being committed to prison for a fine he cannot pay.

He has brought sorrow and disgrace upon his parents, no eye brightens at the mention of his name. Alas! he is a specimen of the "homeless boy" of whom his neighbours the minstrels will sing to-morrow. He is silent and moody, for he is not in funds. Are there none among the company whom sheer misfortune has brought down into this underworld? we ask. Aye, there are, for in this kitchen there are representatives of all sorts and conditions. See that man in the corner by himself, speaking to no one, cooking nothing, eating nothing; he is thinking, thinking! This is his first night in a common lodging-house; it is all new to him, he thinks it all so terrible and disgusting.

He seems inclined to run and spend his night in the streets, and perhaps it will be well for him to do so. He looks decent, bewildered and sorrowful; we know at a glance that some misfortune has tripped him up, we see that self-respect is not dead within him. We know that if he stays the night, breathing the foul air, listening to the horrid talk, seeing much and realising more, feeling himself attacked on every side by the ordinary pests of common lodging-houses, we know that tomorrow morning his self-respect will be lessened, his moral power weakened, and his hope of social recovery almost gone. Let him stay a few weeks, then the lodging-house will become his home and his joy. So we feel inclined to cry out and warn him to escape with his life. This is the great evil and danger of common lodging-houses; needful as they undoubtedly are for the homeless and the outcast, they place the unfortunate on an inclined plane down which they slide to complete demoralisation.

I am told that there are four hundred large common lodging-houses in London, many of them capable of holding several hundred lodgers, and which night after night are filled with a weird collection of humanity. And they cast a fatal spell upon all who get accustomed to them. Few, very few who have become acclimatised ever go back to settled home life. For the decencies, amenities and restraints of citizenship become distasteful. And truly there is much excitement in the life for excitement, at any rate, abounds in common lodging-houses.

Nothing happens in them but the unexpected, and that brings its joys and terrors, its laughter and its tears. Here a great deal of unrestrained human nature is given free play, and the results are exciting if not edifying. Let us spend an evening, but not a night—that is too much to ask-with the habitués.

We sit apart and listen to the babel of voices, but we listen in vain for the lodging-house slang of which we are told so much. They speak very much like other people, and speak on subjects upon which other people speak. They get as excited as ordinary people, too.

Yonder is a lewd fellow shouting obscenities to a female, who, in an equally loud voice and quite as unmistakable language, returns him a Roland for every Oliver.

Here are a couple of wordy excitable fellows who are arguing the pros and cons of Free Trade and Tariff Reform. They will keep at it till the lights are put out, for both are supplied with a plentiful supply of contradictory literature. Both have fluent tongues, equally bitter, and, having their audience, they, like other people, must contend for mastery. Not that they care for the rights or wrongs of either question, for both are prepared, as occasion serves, to take either side. Religion, too, is excitedly discussed, for an animated couple are discussing Christian Evidences, while the ventriloquist gives parsons generally and bishops in particular a very warm time; even the Pope and General Booth do not escape his scurrilous but witty indictments.

Meanwhile the street singers are practising songs, sacred and secular, and our friend the street minstrel produces an old flute and plays an obbligato, whilst the quivering voice of his poor old wife again wants to know the whereabouts of her wandering boy.

There will be a touching scene when they do meet—may I be there! but I hope they will not meet in a common lodging-house. Another street minstrel is practising new tunes upon a mouth-organ, wherewith to soften the hearts of a too obdurate public.

What a babel it all makes; now groups of card-players are getting quarrelsome, for luck has been against some, or cheating has been discovered; blows are exchanged, and blood flows! As the night advances, men and women under the influence of drink arrive. Some are merry, others are quarrelsome, some are moody and lachrymose. The latter become the butt of the former, the noise increases, confusion itself becomes confounded, and we leave to avoid the general MELEE, and to breathe the night air, which we find grateful and reviving. Phew! but it was hot and thick, we don't want to breathe it again. It is astonishing that people get used to it, and like it too! But it leaves its taint upon them, for it permeates their clothing; they carry it about with them, and any one who gets a whiff of it gets some idea of the breath of a common lodging-house. And its moral breath has its effect, too! Woe to all that is fresh and fair, young and hopeful, that comes within its withering influence. Farewell! a long farewell to honour, truth and self-respect, for the hot breath of a common lodging-house will blast those and every other good quality in young people of either sex that inhale it. Its breath comes upon them, and lo! they become foul without and vile within, carrying their moral and physical contagion with them wherever they go.

A moral sepulchre, or rather crematorium, is the common lodging-house, for when its work is done, nothing is left but ashes. For the old habitués I am not much concerned, and though generally I hold a brief for old sinners, criminals and convicts, I hold no brief for the old and middle-aged habitués of a common lodging-house.

Can any one call the dead to life? Can any one convert cold flesh into warm pulsing life? Nay, nay! Talk about being turned into a pillar of salt! the common lodging-house can do more and worse than that! It can turn men and women into pillars of moral death, for even the influence of a long term of penal servitude, withering as it is, cannot for one moment be compared with the corrupting effect of common lodging-house life.

So the old minstrels may go seeking their wandering boy! and the begging-letter writers may go hang!

The human vultures that prey upon the simple and good-natured may, if middle-aged, continue in their evil ways. But what of the young people of whom there ought to be hope? What of them? how long are these "lazar houses" to stand with open door waiting to receive, swallow, transform and eject young humanity? But there is money in them, of course there is; there always is money to be made out of sin and misery if the community permits.

Human wreckage pays, and furnishes a bigger profit than more humdrum investments. I am told by an old habitué with whom I have had endless talks and who has taught me much, although he is a grace-less rascal, that one man owns eight of these large establishments, and that he and his family live in respectability and wealth.

I have no reason to doubt his statement, for these places are mines of wealth, but the owners take precious good care not to live in them. And infinite care that their families do not inhabit them. Some day when we are wise—but wisdom comes so slowly—these things will not be left to private enterprise, for municipalities will provide and own them at no loss to the ratepayers either.

Then decency, though homeless, will have a chance of survival, and moral and physical cleanliness some chance to live, even in a common lodging-house.

Sadly we need a modern St.George who will face and destroy this monstrous dragon with the fiery breath.

Let it not be said that I am unduly hard upon them who from choice or misfortune inhabit these places. From my heart I pity them, but one cannot be blind to the general consequences. And these things must be taken into consideration when efforts are made, as undoubtedly efforts will some day be made, to tackle this question in a reasonable way.

It is high time, too, that the public understood the difficulties that attend any effort to lift lodging-house habitués to a higher form of existence.

I am bold enough to hazard the statement that the number of these people increases year by year, and that no redemptive effort has had the slightest effect in checking the continual increase. As Secretary of the Howard Association, it is my business year by year to make myself acquainted with the criminal statistics, and all matters connected with our prisons. These statistics more than confirm my statement, for they tell us that while drunkenness, brutality, crimes of violence show a steady decrease, vagabondage, sleeping out, begging, etc., show a continual increase as years roll by.

Of course many of them appear again and again in the prison statistics, nevertheless they form a great and terrible army, whose increase bodes ill for dear and fair old England.

Like birds they are migratory, but they pour no sweetness on the morning or evening air. Like locusts they leave a blight behind.

Like famished wolves when winter draws near they seek the habitations of men. Food they must have! There is corn in Egypt!

When gentle spring returns, then heigho! for the country lanes, villages and provincial towns, and as they move from place to place they leave their trail behind them.

And what a trail it is! ask the governors of our local prisons, ask the guardians of any country districts, ask the farmers, aye, and ask the timid women and pretty children, and, my word for it, they will be able to tell you much of these strange beings that returning summer brings unfailingly before them. Their lodging is sometimes the cold hard ground, or the haystack, or perchance, if in luck, an outbuilding.

The prisons are their sanatoria, the workhouses their homes of rest, and the casual ward their temporary conveniences. But always before them is one objective, for a common lodging-house is open to them, and its hypnotism draws them on and on.

So on they go, procreating as they go. Carrying desolation with them, leaving desolation behind them. The endurance of these people—I suppose they must be called people—is marvellous and their rate of progression is sometimes astonishing; weary and footsore, maimed, halt or blind they get over the ground at a good uniform pace.

Look at that strange being that has just passed us as we sat on the bank of a country lane; he goes along with slouching gait and halting steps; he has no boots worthy of the name, his tattered trousers, much too long, give us glimpses of his flesh. He wears an old frock-coat that hangs almost to his heels, and a cloth cap, greasy and worn, upon his head. His beard is wild and abundant, and his hair falls upon his shoulders in a way worthy of an artist or poet.

Follow him, but not too closely, and you will find it hard to keep up with him, he knows what he is making for. Neither George Borrow nor Runciman would hold him for a week, for George would want to stop and talk, but this fellow is silent and grim. A lazar house draws him on, and he needs must reach it, weak and ill-fed though he is!

And he will reach others too, for he is on a circular tour. But next winter will find him in a Westminster lodging-house if he has luck, on the Embankment if he has not.

He has an easy philosophy: "All the things in the world belong to all the men in the world," is his outspoken creed, so he steals when he can, and begs when he cannot steal.

But think of this life when women share it, and children are born into it, and lads and lassies are on the tramp. Dare we think of it? We dare not! If we did, it would not be tolerated for a day. Neither dare I write about it, for there are many things that cannot be written. So I leave imagination to supply what words must not convey.

But it is all so pitiful, it is too much for me, for sometimes I feel that I am living with them, tramping with them, sleeping with them, eating with them; I am become as one of them. I feel the horror, yet I do not realise the charms.

I am an Englishman! I love liberty! I must be free, or die! I want to order my own life, to control my own actions, to run on my own lines; I would that all men should have similar rights. But, alas! it cannot be—civilisation claims and enchains us; we have to submit to its discipline, and it is well that it should be so. We do not, cannot live to ourselves, and for ourselves. Those days have long passed, and for ever. Orderly life and regular duties are good for us, and necessary for the well-being of the nation.

A strong robust: nation demands and requires a large amount of freedom, and this it must have, or perish! The individual man, too, requires a fair amount if he is to be a man. But we may, and we do in some things extend freedom beyond the legitimate bounds. For in a country of limited area where the bulk of the people live onerous lives, and manfully perform their duties, we allow a host of parasites to thrive and swarm.

The more this host increases, the weaker the nation becomes, and its existence may ultimately become not a sign of freedom but a proof of national decay. For parasites thrive on weakly life, be it individual or national. So while we have a profound pity for the nomads, let us express it with a strong hand. They cannot care for themselves in any decent way. Let us care for them, and detain them in places that will allow permanent detention and segregation. And the results will be surprising, for prisons will be less numerous, workhouses, casual wards and asylums less necessary, lazar houses with their pestilential breath will pass away, and England will be happier, sweeter and more free!

V

Furnished Apartments

What fell power decreed that certain streets in London should be devoted to the purpose of providing "furnished apartments" for the submerged I do not know. But I do know that some streets are entirely devoted to this purpose, and that a considerable amount of money is made out of such houses.

I ask my readers to accompany me for a visit to one of these streets, and make some acquaintance with the houses, the furniture and the inhabitants.

The particular streets we select run at a right-angle from a main thoroughfare, a railway divides them from a beautiful park, and on this railway City merchants pass daily to and from their suburban homes.

I question whether in the whole of London more misery, vice and poverty can be found located in one limited area than in the streets we are about to visit. I know them, and I have every reason for knowing them. We make our visit in summer time, when poverty is supposed to be less acute. As we enter the street we notice at once that a commodious public-house stands and thrives at the entrance. We also notice that there are in the street several "general" shops, where tea and margarine, firewood, pickles, paraffin oil and cheese, boiled ham and vinegar, corned beef and Spanish onions, bread and matches are to be obtained.

We stand in the middle of the roadway, in the midst of dirt and refuse, and look up and down the street. Innumerable children are playing in the gutter or on the pavements, and the whole place teems with life. We observe that the houses are all alike, the shops excepted. They stand three-storey high; there are nine rooms in each house. We look in vain for bright windows and for clean and decent curtains.

Every room seems occupied, for there is no card in any window announcing "furnished apartments." The street is too well known to require advertisement, consequently the "furnished apartments" are seldom without tenants.

The street is a cave of Adullam to which submerged married couples resort when their own homes, happy or otherwise, are broken up.

We notice that it is many days since the doors and window-frames of the different houses made acquaintance with the painter. We notice that all doors stand open, for it is nobody's business to answer a knock, friendly or otherwise. We look in the various doorways and see in each case the same sort of staircase and the same unclean desolation.

Who would believe that Adullam Street is a veritable Tom Tiddler's Ground? Would any one believe that a colony of the submerged could prove a source of wealth?

Let us count the houses on both sides of the street. Forty-five houses! Leave out the two "general" shops, the greengrocer's and the "off licence"; leave out also the one where the agent and collector lives, that leaves us forty-one houses of nine rooms let out as furnished apartments.

If let to married couples that means a population of seven hundred and thirty-eight, if all the rooms are occupied, and supposing that no couple occupies more than one room. As for the children—but we dare not think of them—we realise the advantage of the open street of which we freely grant them the freehold. But we make the acquaintance of a tenant and ask some questions. We find that she has two children, that they have but one furnished room, for which they pay seven shillings and sixpence weekly in advance! Always in advance!

She further tells us that their room is one of the best and largest; it faces the street, and is on the first floor. She says that some rooms are let at six shillings, others at six shillings and sixpence, and some at seven shillings. We ask her why she lives in Adullam Street, and she tells us that her own furniture was obtained on the "hire system," and when it was seized they came to Adullam Street, and they do not know how they are to get out of it.

That sets us thinking and calculating; three hundred and sixty-nine rooms, rent always payable in advance—from the submerged, too!—average six shillings and sixpence per week per room, why, that is L120 per week, or L6,240 annually from forty-one houses, if they are regularly occupied. Truly furnished apartments specially provided for the submerged are extra specially adapted to the purpose of keeping them submerged.

As no deputy disputes our entrance, we enter and proceed to gain some knowledge of the tenants, and take some stock of their rooms and furniture.

The rooms are simply but by no means sweetly furnished! Here is an inventory and a mental picture of one room. A commodious bed with dirty appointments that makes us shudder! A dirty table on which are some odds and ends of unclean crockery, a couple of cheap Windsor chairs, a forbidding-looking chest of drawers, a rusty frying-pan, a tin kettle, a teapot and a common quart jug. He would be a bold man that bid ten shillings for the lot, unless he bought them as a going concern. A cheap and nasty paper covers the wall, excepting where pieces have been torn away, and the broken walls are made of lath and plaster, to provide splendid cover for innumerable insects which remain in undisputed possession.

One floor much resembles another, but the basement and the top storey rooms are the worst of all. We look through the window of a second floor back room, and see the out premises, but one look is sufficient.

We want to know something of the tenants, so we enter into conversation with them, and find them by no means reserved.

Room 1. Husband and wife about thirty-five years of age, no children; husband has been ill for some months, during which the rent got behind. When he was taken to the infirmary they lost their home altogether; she did washing and charing for a time, but ultimately got into the "House."

When her husband got better, and was discharged from the infirmary, his old mates collected ten shillings for him, he took the room in which they now lived, and of course she joined him.

How did they live? Well, it was hardly living; her husband looked round every day and managed to "pick up something," and she got a day or two days' work every week—their rent was always paid in advance. What happened when her husband did not "pick up something" she did not say, but semi-starvation seemed the only alternative.

No. 2. Husband, wife and a girl of seven engaged in making coarse paper flowers of lurid hue. They had been in that room for six months; they sold the paper flowers in the streets, but being summer time they did not sell many. At Christmas time people bought them for decorations; sometimes people gave the girl coppers, but did not take the flowers from her. The police watched them very closely, as they required a licence for selling, and if they took the girl out in the wet or dark the police charged them.

It was very difficult to live at all, owing to police interference. The girl did not go to school, but they had been warned that she must go; they did not know what they should do when she could not help them.

Room 3. A strong man about thirty, his wife and two young children. The remains of a meal upon the table, a jug of beer and a smell of tobacco. The man looks at us, and a flash of recognition is exchanged. He had been released from prison at 8.30 that morning after serving a sentence of nine months for shop robbery.

We asked how much gratuity he had earned. Eight shillings, he told us. His wife and children had met him at the prison gate; they had come straight to that room, for which the wife had previously arranged; they had paid a week in advance. "What was he going to do?" "He did not know!" He did not appear to care, but he supposed he "must look round, he would get the rent somehow." We felt that he spoke the truth, and that he would "get the rent somehow" till the police again prevented him.

We know that prison will again welcome him, and that the workhouse gates will open to receive his wife and children, the number of which will increase during his next detention in prison.

Room 4. Two females under thirty. No signs of occupation; they are not communicative, neither are they rude, so we learn nothing from them except that they were not Londoners.

Room 5. A family group, father, mother and four children; they had come to Adullam Street because they had been ejected from their own home. Their goods and chattels had been put on the street pavement, whence the parish had removed them to the dust destructor, probably the best thing to do with them.

The family were all unhealthy and unclean. The parents did not seem to have either strength, grit or intelligence to fit them for any useful life. But they could creep forth and beg, the woman could stand in the gutter with a little bit of mortality wrapped in her old shawl, for tender-hearted passers-by to see its wizened face, and the father could stand not far away from her with a few bootlaces or matches exposed, as if for sale. They managed to live somehow.

Room 6. An elderly couple who had possessed no home of their own for years past, but who know London well, for the furnished lodgings of the east, west, north and south are familiar to them.

He sells groundsel, she sells water-cress, at least they tell us so, and point to baskets as evidence. But we know that groundsel business of old. We have seen him standing in a busy thoroughfare with his pennyworth of groundsel, and we know that though he receives many pennies his stock remains intact, and we know also that pennyworths of water-cress in the dirty hands of an old woman serve only the same purpose.

Room 7. Here we find a younger but not more hopeful couple; she is fairly well dressed, and he is rather flashy. They have both food and drink. We know that when the shades of night fall she will be perambulating the streets, and he like a beast of prey will be watching not far away. So we might go through the whole of the colony. There is a strange assortment of humanity in Adullam Street. Vice and misery, suffering and poverty, idleness and dishonesty, feeble-mindedness and idiocy are all blended, but no set-off in virtue and industry is to be found.

The strong rogue lives next to the weak and the unfortunate, the hardened old sinner next door to some who are beginning to qualify for a like old age. The place is coated with dirt and permeated with sickening odours. And to Adullam Street come young couples who have decided to unite their lives and fortunes without any marriage ceremony; for in Adullam Street such unions abound.

Young fellows of nineteen earning as much as twelve shillings a week couple with girls of less age earning ten shillings weekly. It looks so easy to live on twenty-two shillings a week and no furniture to buy, and no parson to pay.

So a cheap ring is slipped on, and hand in hand the doomed couple go to Adullam Street, which receives them with open arms, and hugs them so long as six shillings and sixpence weekly is forthcoming in advance. Their progress is very rapid; when the first child arrives, the woman's earnings cease, and Adullam Street knows them no more.

Ticket-of-leave men, ex-convicts, heroes of many convictions, come to Adullam Street and bring their female counterparts with them. They flourish for a time, and then the sudden but not unexpected disappearance of the male leads to the disappearance of the female. She returns to her former life; Adullam Street is but an incident in her life.

So there is a continual procession through Adullam Street; very little good enters it, and it is certain that less good passes out.

Where do its temporary inhabitants go? To prisons, to workhouses, to hospitals, to common lodging-houses, to shelters, to the Embankment and to death.

Although those who seek sanctuary in Adullam Street are already inhabitants of the underworld, a brief sojourn in it dooms them to lower depths. I suppose there must be places of temporary residence for the sort of people that inhabit it, for they must have shelter somewhere. But I commend this kind of property to the searching eyes of the local authorities and the police.

But furnished apartments can tell another tale when they are not situated in Adullam Street. For sometimes a struggling widow, or wife with a sick husband, or a young married couple seek to let furnished apartments as a legitimate means of income. When they do so, let them beware of the underworld folk who happen to be better clothed and more specious than their fellows, or they will bitterly rue it.

Very little payment will they get. Couples apparently married and apparently respectable, but who are neither, are common enough, who are continually on the look-out for fresh places of abode, where they may continue their depredation.

They are ready enough with a deposit, but that is all the money they mean to part with, and that has probably been raised by robbing their last landlady. They can give references if required, and show receipts, too, from their last lodgings, for they carry rent-books made out by themselves and fully paid up for the purpose. They are adepts at obtaining entrance, and, once in, they remain till they have secured another place and marked another prey.

Meanwhile their poor victims suffer in kind and money, and are brought nearer destitution. I have frequently known a week's rent paid with the part proceeds of articles stolen from either the furnished apartments, or some other part of the house just entered.

I could tell some sad stories of suffering and distress brought to struggling and decent people by these pests, of whom a great number are known to the police.

And so the merry game goes on, for while vampires are sucking the impure blood of the wretched dwellers in Adullam Street lodgings, the dwellers in Adullam Street in their turn prey on the community at large.

Meanwhile the honest and unfortunate poor can scarcely find cover, and when they do, why, then their thin blood is drained, for they have to pay exorbitantly.

It is apparently easy to transmute wretched humanity into gold. But who is going to call order out of this horrid chaos? No one, I am thinking, for no one seems to dare attempt in any thorough way to solve the question of housing the very poor, and that question lies at the root of this matter.

Let any one attempt it, and a thousand formidable vested interests rise up and confront him, against which he will dash himself in vain. As to housing the inhabitants of the underworld at a reasonable rental, no one seems to have entertained the idea.

Lease holders and sub-lease holders, landlords and ground landlords, corporations and churches, philanthropists and clergymen have all got vested interests in house property where wretchedness and dirt are conspicuous. "But," said a notable clergyman in regard to some horrid slum, "I cannot help it, I have only a life-interest in it," as if, forsooth, he could have more; did he wish to carry his interests beyond the grave? I would give life-interest in rotten house property short shrift by burning the festering places. But such places are not burned, though sometimes they are closed by the order of the local authorities. But oftener still they are purchased by local authorities at great public cost, or by philanthropic trusts. Then the human rabbits are driven from their warrens to burrow elsewhere and so leave room for respectability.

Better-looking and brighter buildings are erected where suites of rooms are to let at very high prices. Then a tax is placed upon children, and a premium is offered to sterility. Glowing accounts appear in the Press, and royalty goes to inspect the new gold mine! We rub our hands with complacent satisfaction and say, "Ah! at last something is being done for housing the very poor!" But what of the rabbits! have they ascended to the seventh heaven of the new paradise? Not a bit; they cannot offer the required credentials, or pay the exorbitant rent! not for them seven flights of stone stairs night and morning; it is so much easier for rabbits to burrow underground, or live in the open. So away they scuttle! Some to dustheaps, some back to Adullam Street, some to nomadic life. But most of them to other warrens, to share quarters with other rabbits till those warrens in their turn are converted into "dwellings," when again they must needs scuttle and burrow elsewhere.

Can it be wondered at that these people are dirty and idle; and that many of them ultimately prefer the settled conditions of prison or workhouse life, or take to vagrancy?

I cannot find a royal specific for this evil; humanity will, under any conditions, have its problems and difficulties. Vagrants have always existed, and probably will continue to exist while the human race endures. But we need not manufacture them! Human rookeries and rabbit warrens must go; England, little England, cannot afford them, and ought not to tolerate them. But before we dispossess the rooks and the rabbits, let us see to it that, somewhere and somehow, cleaner nests and sweeter holes are provided for them. The more I think upon this question the more I am convinced that it is the great question of the day, and upon its solution the future of our country depends.

See what is happening! Thousands of children born to this kind of humanity become chargeable to the guardians or find entrance to the many children's homes organised by philanthropy. One course is taken the bright and healthy, the sound in body and mind, are emigrated; but the smitten, the afflicted, the feeble and the worthless are kept at home to go through the same life, to endure the same conditions as their parents, and in their turn to produce a progeny that will burrow in warrens or scuttle out of them even as their parents did before them.

But the feebler the life, the greater the progeny; this we cannot escape, for Nature will take care of herself. We, may drive out the rabbits, we may imprison and punish them, we may compel them to live in Adullam Street or in lazar houses, we may harry them and drive them hither and thither, we may give them doles of food on the Embankment or elsewhere. We may give them chopping wood for a day, we may lodge them for a time in labour homes; all this we may do, but we cannot uplift them by these methods. We cannot exterminate them. But by ignoring them we certainly give them an easy chance of multiplying to such a degree that they will constitute a national danger.

VI

The Disabled

In this chapter I want to speak of those who suffer from physical disabilities, either from birth, the result of accident, or disease. If this great army of homeless afflicted humanity were made to pass in procession before us, it would, I venture to say, so touch our hearts that we should not want the procession repeated.

Nothing gives us more pleasure than the sight of a number of people who, suffering from some one or other physical deprivation, are being taught some handicraft by which they will be able to earn a modest living.

Probably nothing causes us greater sadness than the sight of deformed and crippled men and women who are utterly unable to render any useful service to the community, and who consequently have to depend upon their wits for a miserable living. It is a very remarkable thing that an accident which deprives a man of a leg, of an arm, or of eyesight, not only deprives him of his living, but also frequently produces a psychological change. And unless some counterbalancing conditions serve to influence in an opposite direction he may become dangerous. It was not without reason that our older novelists made dwarfs and hunchbacks to be inhuman fiends. Neither was it without reason that Dickens, our great student of human nature, made of Quilp a twisted dwarf, and Stagg a blind man his most dangerous characters. Some years ago I was well acquainted with a very decent man, a printer; he had lived for years beyond reproach; he was both a good workman, husband and father. But he lost his right arm, the result of an accident at his work, and his character changed from that day. He became morose, violent and cruel, and obsessed with altogether false ideas. He could not reason as other men, and he became dangerous and explosive. Time after time I have seen him committed to prison, until he became a hopeless prison habitué. My experience has also shown me that physical deprivations are equally likely to lead to sharpened wits and perverted moral sense as to explosive and cruel violence. Probably this is natural, for nature provides some compensation to those who suffer loss.

This is what makes the army of the physically handicapped so dangerous. The disabled must needs live, and their perverted moral sense and sharpened wits enable them to live at the expense of the public.

Very clever, indeed, many of these men are; they know how to provoke pity, and they know how to tell a plausible tale. Many of them can get money without even asking for it. They know full well the perils that environ the man who begs. I am not ashamed to say that I have been frequently duped by such fellows, and have learned by sad experience that my wits cannot cope with theirs, and that my safety lies in hasty retreat when they call upon me, for I have always found that conversation with them leads to my own undoing.

Witness the following. One winter night my eldest son, who lives about a mile away, went out to post a letter at midnight. After dropping his letter in the pillar-box, he was surprised to hear a voice say, "Will you kindly show me the way to Bridlington?" "Bridlington! why, it is more than two hundred miles away." The request made my son gasp, for, as I have said, it was winter and midnight.

The audacity of the request, however, arrested his attention, and that doubtless was the end to be secured. So a conversation followed. The inquirer was a Scotchman about thirty years of age; he wore dark glasses and was decently clad; he had been discharged from St. Bartholomew's Hospital. He was a seaman, but owing to a boiler explosion on board he had been treated in the hospital. Now he must walk to Bridlington, where an uncle lived who would give him a home. He produced a letter from his uncle, but he had either lost or torn up the envelope. All this and more he told my son with such candour and sincerity, that he was soon the poorer by half-a-crown. Then, to improve the fellow's chance of getting to Bridlington, he brought him to me. I was enjoying my beauty sleep when that ill-fated knock aroused me. Donning a warm dressing-gown and slippers, I went down to the front door, and very soon the three of us were shivering round the remains of a fire in my dining-room.

Very lucidly and modestly Angus repeated the above story, not once did he falter or trip. He showed me the letter from his uncle, he pointed out the condition of his eyes and the scars on his face; with some demur he accepted my half-crown, saying that he did not ask for anything, and that all he wanted was to get to Bridlington.

In my pyjamas and dressing-gown I explored the larder and provided him with food, after which my son escorted him to the last tramcar, saw him safely on his way to the Seamen's Institute with a note to the manager guaranteeing the expense of his bed and board for a few days.

Next day my son visited the Seamen's Institute, but alas! Angus was not there, he had not been there. Nevertheless the manager knew something of him, for three separate gentlemen had sent Angus to the institute. One had found him in the wilds of Finchley looking for Bridlington! Another had found him pursuing the same quest at Highgate, while still another had come on him, with his dark glasses, bundle and stick, looking for Bridlington on the road to Southgate.

I do not know whether the poor fellow ever arrived at Bridlington, but this I do know, that he has found his way northwards, and that he is now groping and inquiring for Dawlish in Devonshire.

The Manchester Guardian tells us that one silent evening hour poor Angus was discovered in several different places in the vicinity of Manchester. The same paper of the next day's date stated that eleven out of the twelve who met poor Angus were so overcome by the poignancy of his narrative and the stupendous character of his task, that they promptly gave him financial assistance. I am strongly of the opinion that the twelfth man was entirely without money at the time he met Angus, or I feel that he would have proved no exception to the rule. In my heart I was glad to find that the hard-headed citizens of Manchester are just as kind-hearted and likely to be imposed upon as we are in London.

But Angus has been playing his fame for six years at least, for one gentleman who gave him explicit directions more than five years ago writes to the Manchester Guardian saying, "I am afraid he took a wrong turning."

It is evident that Angus has done fairly well at his business, and yet it would appear that he never asked for a single penny since he first started on his endless search. He always accepts money reluctantly, and I much question whether the police have right to arrest him, or the gulled public any ground to complain.

But if Angus should ever get to his kind uncle at Bridlington, and that respected gentleman should return the five shillings we gave to help his unfortunate nephew, I will promise to be more careful in pressing money upon strangers in future. But whether the money comes to hand or not I have made myself a promise, and it is this: never more to get out of a warm bed on a cold night to open the house and entertain a half-blind man that speaks with a rich Scotch accent.

But how clever it all is! Why, its very audacity ensures its success, and Angus, for aught I know, has many fellow-craftsmen. Certainly if he is alone he must be almost ubiquitous. But Angus and such-like are not to be wondered at, for Nature herself endows all living things with the powers to adapt themselves to circumstances and obtain the means of defence and offence from their conditions. So Nature deals with the human family, in whom the struggle for existence develops varied, powerful and maybe dangerous characteristics.

At present it is nobody's business to see that the maimed, the halt, the blind are taught and trained to be of some service, and made able in some way to earn a subsistence. Philanthropy, it is true, does something, and also those blessed institutions, the schools for the blind, and training homes for the crippled. I never see such institutions without experiencing great gladness, for I know how much evil they avert. But the great body of the physically afflicted are without the walls and scope of these institutions, consequently tens of thousands of men and women, because of their afflictions, are enabled to prey upon the community with a cunning that other people cannot emulate.

We hear daily of accidents. We learn of men and women losing arms, legs and hands; our hearts are touched for a brief moment, then we remember the particulars no more. The ultimate consequences are unseen, but they are not to be avoided, for every cripple left uncared for may become a criminal of dangerous type.

Their elemental needs and passions still exist, notwithstanding their physical deprivations. They claim the right to eat and drink, they claim the right of perpetuating their kind.

Some day perhaps the community will realise what the exercise of the latter right means. Some day, and Heaven send that day soon, we shall be horrified at the thought that a vast number of unfortunates exist among us who, demanding our pity and our care, are going down to the grave without that care to which their physical disabilities entitle them.

As we look at these unfortunates, feelings of pity, disgust or amusement may be aroused, but one moment's reflection would convince us that these afflicted homeless creatures manage to exist and extort an expensive living from the community.

I have said that every disabled man is a potential criminal, and that unless he receives some compensation giving him the means of earning honestly his living, he is certain to be a danger or a parasite. This is but natural, for in the first place his physical nature has received a shock, has sustained an outrage, Nature strikes back, and some one has to suffer. The loss of a limb means severed muscles, bones and nerves. Nature never forgets that they ought to be there, but as they are not there she does without them; but none the less she feels for them instinctively, and becomes disappointed and bitter because she is refused the use of them.

Add to this the anxiety, the sufferings the amputated man feels when he is also deprived of his means of livelihood, as well as his limb, and from comfort comes down to penury. Perhaps he has been able hitherto to keep his wife and children with a fair amount of comfort; now he is helpless and has to depend upon them.

He may be of proud spirit, but he has to endure mortification by seeing his wife labour and slave for him. He becomes moody, then passionate, a little drink maddens him, then comes the danger. He does something, then the police are required, and prison awaits him. There he thinks and broods over his wrong, with bitterness and revengeful spirit. Perhaps his wife has been compelled to give evidence against him; he remembers that, he scores it up, and henceforth there is no peace for either of them!

Frequent convictions follow, ultimately the wife has to claim the protection of the law, and gets a separation order on account of his cruelty. Henceforward he is an outcast, his children and friends cast him off, for they are afraid of him. But he lives on, and many have to suffer because he has lost a limb.

We read a great deal about the development of character through suffering, and well I know the purifying effects suffering has upon our race; but it is well sometimes to look at the reverse side, and consider what evil follows in the wake of suffering.

Blind men, the deaf and the dumb and the physically disabled need our pitiful consideration. Some of the sweetest, cleverest, bravest men I know suffer from great physical disabilities, but they have pleasures and compensations, they live useful lives, their compensations have produced light and sweetness, they are not useless in a busy world, they are not mere cumberers of the ground. They were trained for usefulness whilst they were young.

But a far different case is presented with the disabled among the very poor. What chance in life is there for a youth of twenty who loses an arm or leg? He has no friends whose loving care and whose financial means can soften his affliction and keep him in comfort while training for service. Who in this rich, industrial England wants such service as he can render? Very few! and those who do make use of him naturally feel that his service is not worth much.

Numbers of my acquaintances like Angus half lose their sight! Who requires their service? No one! But these men live on, and they mean to live on, and Nature furnishes them with the means by giving them extra cunning. Many of these fellows, poor disabled fellows, inhabit the dark places of the underworld. Let us call them out of their dark places and number them, classify them, note their disabilities!

Truly they came down to the underworld through great afflictions. They form the disabled army of civilisation's industrial world who have been wounded and crippled in the battle. All sorts of accidents have happened to them: explosions have blinded them, steam has scalded them, buffers have crushed them, coal has buried them, trains have run over them, circular saws have torn them asunder. They are bent and they are twisted, they are terrible to look at; as we gaze at them we are fascinated. March! now see them move! Did you ever see anything like this march of disabled men from the gloom of the underworld?

How they shuffle and drag along; what strange, twisted and jerky movements they have; what sufferings they must endure, and what pain they must have had. All these thoughts come to us as we look at the march of the disabled as they twist and writhe past us.

The procession is endless, for it is continually augmented by men and women from the upperworld, who as conscripts are sent to the army below, because they have sustained injuries in the service of the world above.

So they pass! But the upperworld has not done with them; it does not get rid of its natural obligations so easily. It suffers with them, and pays dearly for its neglect of them. The disabled live on, they will not die to please us, and they extract a pretty expensive living from the world above. The worst of it is that these unfortunates prey also upon those who have least to spare, the respectable poor just above the line. They do not always sit at the gates of the rich asking for crumbs, for the eloquence of their afflictions and the pity of their woes strike home to the hearts and pockets of the industrious poor who have so little to spare. But it is always much easier to rob the poor!

It is our boast that Englishmen love justice, and it is a true boast! But when we read of accidents and of surgical operations, does our imagination lead us to ask: What about the future of the sufferers? Very rarely, I expect.

The fact is, we have got so used to this sight of maimed manhood that it causes us but little anxious thought, though it may cause some feelings of revulsion.

But there is the Employers' Liability Act! Yes, I admit it, and a blessed Act it is. But the financial consideration given for a lost limb or a ruined body is not a fortune; it soon evaporates, then heigho! for the underworld, for bitterness and craft.

But all accidents do not come within the scope of that Act, not by any means. If a married woman about to become a mother falls or rolls down the stairs, when climbing to her home in the seventh heaven of Block-land, if she sustains long injuries, who compensates her? If the child is born a monstrosity, though not an idiot, who compensates for that? If the poor must be located near the sky, how is it that "lifts" cannot be provided for them? Who can tell the amount of maimed child, middle-aged and elderly life that has resulted from the greasy stairs and dark landings of London dwellings. Industrial life, commercial life and social life take a rare toll of flesh and blood from the poor. For this civilisation makes no provision excepting temporary sustentation in hospitals, workhouses or prisons. Even our prison commissioners tell us that "our prisons are largely filled with the very poor, the ignorant, the feeble, the incapable and the incapacitated."

It would appear that if we can make no other provision for the disabled, we can make them fast in prison for a time. But that time soon passes, and their poor life is again resumed. But the disabled are not the only suffering unfortunates in the netherworld who, needing our pity, receive the tender mercies of prison. For there epileptics abide or roam in all the horror of their lives "oft-times in water and oft-times in the fire," a burden to themselves, a danger to others. Shut out from industrial life and shut out from social life. Refused lodgings here and refused lodgings there. Sometimes anticipating fits, sometimes recovering from fits; sometimes in a semi-conscious state, sometimes in a state of madness. Never knowing what may happen to them, never knowing what they may do to others. Always suffering, always hopeless! Treated as criminals till their deeds are fatal, then certified to be "criminal lunatics." Such is the life of the underworld epileptic. Life, did I call it?—let me withdraw that word; it is the awful, protracted agony of a living death, in which sanity struggles with madness, rending and wounding a poor human frame. Happy are they when they die young! but even epileptics live on and on; but while they live we consign them to the underworld, where their pitiful cry of "Woe! woe!" resounds.

Do not say this is an exaggeration, for it is less than truth, not beyond it. Poe himself, with all his imagination and power, could not do full justice to this matter.

Mendicity societies in their report tell of cunning rascals who impose on the public by simulating "fits"; they tell of the "king of fits," the "soap fits king," and others. They point with some satisfaction to the convictions of these clever rogues, and claim some credit in detecting them.

Their statements are true! But why are they true? Because real epileptics are so common in the underworld, and their sufferings so palpable and striking, that parasites, even though afflicted themselves, nay, because of their own disabilities, can and do simulate the weird sufferings of epileptics. Will mendicity societies, when they tell us about, enumerate for us, and convict for us the hoary impostors, also tell us about and enumerate for us the stricken men and women who are not impostors, and whose fits are unfortunately genuine?

If some society will do this, they will do a great public service; but at present no one does it, so this world of suffering, mystery and danger remains unexplored.

I do not wonder that the ancients thought that epileptics suffered from demoniacal possessions; perhaps they do, perhaps we believe so still. At any rate we deal with them in pretty much the same way as in days of old. The ancients bound them with chains; we are not greatly different—we put them in prison. The ancients did allow their epileptics to live in the tombs, but we allow them no place but prison, unless their friends have money!

But let me end the subject by stating that the non-provision for epileptics is a national disgrace and a national danger. That incarceration of epileptics in prison and their conviction as criminals is unjust and cruel. That it is utterly impossible for philanthropy to restrain, detain and care for epileptics. That the State itself must see to the matter!

But just another word: epileptics marry! Imagine if you can the life of a woman married to an epileptic.

Epileptics have children of a sort! Can you imagine what they are likely to be? You cannot! Well, then, I will tell you. Irresponsible beings, with abnormal passions, but with little sense of truth and honour, with no desire for continuous labour, but possessed of great cunning. The girls probably immoral, the boys feckless and drunken.

We have to pay for our neglect; we have no pity upon epileptics. He and his children have no pity for us!

VII

Women in the Underworld

The women of the underworld may be divided into three great classes. Those who by reason of their habits or mental peculiarities prefer to live homeless lives. Secondly, those whom misfortune has deprived of settled home life. Thirdly, those who, having settled homes, live at starvation point.

In London there is a great number of each class. With class one I shall deal briefly, for they do not form a pleasant theme. The best place to study these wild homeless women is Holloway Prison, for here you will find them by the hundreds any day you please. In Holloway Prison during one year 933 women who had been in that gaol more than ten times were again received into it.

I am privileged sometimes to address them. As I write I see them sitting before me. After one of my addresses I was speaking to one of the wardresses about their repeated convictions, when the wardress said—

"Oh, sir, we are glad to see them come back again, for we know that they are far better off with us than they are at liberty. They go out clean and tidy with very much better health than they came in. It seems cruel to let them out, to live again in dirt and misery, and though we have an unpleasant duty to perform in cleansing them when they return, we feel some comfort in the thought that for a short time they will be cared for. Why, sir, it is prison and prison alone that keeps them alive."

Now this army of women is a dolorous army in all truth, for their faces, their figures are alike strange and repulsive, and many of them seem to be clothed with the cerements of moral and spiritual death. They are frequently charged with drunkenness, stealing, begging, or sleeping out.

Their names appear on the "Black List," for the law says they are "habitual inebriates," yet drink has little or nothing to do with their actual condition.

Let any one look them in the face as I have looked them in the face, study their photographs as I have studied them, and I venture to affirm that they will say with me, "These women are not responsible beings." For years I have been drumming this fact into the ears of the public, and at length the authorities acknowledged it, for in 1907 the Home Office Inspector issued a report on inebriate reformatories, and gave the following account of those who had been in such institutions: 2,277 had been treated in reformatories; of these he says 51 were insane and sent to lunatic asylums, 315 others were pronounced defectives or imbeciles. Altogether he tells us that 62 out of every hundred were irresponsible women and unfit for social and industrial life.

My many years' experience of London's underworld confirms the testimony of the Home Office, for I am persuaded that a very large proportion of homeless women on our streets are homeless because they are quite unfitted for, and have no desire for decent social life.

Should I be asked about the birth and parentage of these women, I reply that they come from all classes. Born of tramps and of decent citizens, born in the slums and sometimes in villas, almost every rank and station contributes its quota to this class of wild, hopeless women.

But I pass on to the second class, those who by misfortune have become submerged. This, too, is a large class, and a class more worthy of sympathy and consideration than the others, for amongst them, in spite of misfortune and poverty, there is a great deal of womanliness and self-respect. Misfortune, ill-health, sorrow, loss of money, position or friends, circumstances over which they have had but little or no control have condemned them to live in the underworld. Such women present a pitiful sight and a difficult problem. They cling to the relics of their respectability with a passionate devotion, and they wait, hope, starve and despair.

Often misfortune has come upon them when the days of youth were passed, and they found themselves in middle age faced with the grim necessity of earning a living. I have seen many of them struggle with difficulty, and exhibit rare courage and patience; I have watched them grow older and feebler. Sometimes I have provided glasses that their old eyes might be strengthened for a little needlework, but I have always known that it was only helping to defer the evil day, when they would no longer be able to pay the rent for a little room in a very poor neighbourhood. My mind is charged with the memory of women who have passed through this experience, who from comfortable homes have descended to the underworld to wander with tired feet, weary bodies and hopeless hearts till they lie down somewhere and their wanderings cease for ever.

But before we consider these women, let us take a peep at the lower depths. Come, then! Now we are in a charnel house, for we are down among the drunken women, the dissolute women that stew and writhe in the underworld, for whom there is no balm in Gilead and no physician. Now we realise what moral death means.

Like the horde of Comus they lie prone, and wallow in their impurity. Hot as the atmosphere is, feverish though their defiled bodies be, they call for no friendly hand to give them water to cool their parched throats. The very suggestion of water makes them sick and faint.

But a great cry smites us: "Give us drink! and we will forget our misery; give us drink, and we will sing and dance before you! give us drink, and you may have us body and soul! Drink! drink!" A passionate, yearning, importunate cry everlastingly comes from them for drink.

Now with Dante we are walking in Hell; see, there is a form, half human and half animal, creeping towards us with lewd look and suggestion. Yonder is an old hag fearful to look upon. Here a group of cast-off wives, whom the law has allowed outraged husbands to consign to this perdition; but who, when sober enough, come back to the upperworld and drag others down to share their fate.

Does any one want to know what becomes of the wives who, having developed a love of drink, have been separated from their husbands, and cast homeless into the streets? Here in this circle of Hell you may find them, consigned to a moral death from which there is no resurrection.

And the idle, the vicious, the lustful and the criminal are here too. But we leave them, and get back to the everlasting workers, the sober and virtuous women of whom I have told. What a contrast is here presented! Drunkenness, vice, bestiality and crime! Virtue, industry, honesty and self-respect condemned to live together! But let us look and listen; we hear a voice speaking to us—

"Dear Mr. Holmes, I am deeply interested in your work, and feel one with you in mind and heart in the different troubles of human life, and of their causes and consequences. I feel that if only my health was better, and I was placed in some other sphere of life, that I would do something to help on your good work. But, alas! I shall never be strong again; the hard grinding for a miserable pittance gives me no chance to get nourishing food and recover my strength. Some people say to me, 'Why don't you go into the workhouse or the infirmary?' This I bear in silence, but it is simply killing me in a slow way. Oh! that it should take so long to kill some of us. It makes me sad to think that so many lives are wrecked in this way, that so many are driven to wrong, that so many others should drift away into lives of hopelessness. I have been stripped of all, and I am waiting for the worst."

Can any language beat that for lucidity and pathos? My readers will, I am sure, recognise that those are the words of an educated woman. Yes, her education was begun in England and finished on the Continent. Were I to mention the name of the writer's mother, hearts would leap, for that name lives in story and song.

But her parents died and left no competence, her health failed, and teaching became impossible. All she now requires is an out-patient's ticket for a chest hospital.

She is a "trouser finisher," and earns one penny per hour; sometimes she lies on her bed while at work. But by and by she will not be able to earn her penny per hour; then there will be "homelessness," but not the workhouse for her.

But the voice speaks again: "Dear Mr. Holmes, please excuse me not thanking you sooner for offering me a hospital letter. I shall, indeed, be very grateful for one when able to get about, for I shall need something to set me up a bit.

"At present I am very sadly indeed; my foot seems very much better, yet not right, the sister thinks. To make matters worse, I have a very bad gathered finger, and this week I have not been able to do a stitch of work; indeed, it is very little that I have been able to do this last ten weeks. Oh, the cruel oppression of taking advantage and putting extra work for less pay, because I cannot get out to fetch it myself!

"The most I get is a penny per hour; it is generally less. Sister Grace was so vexed by the rude message he sent to-day while she was here, because I could not do the work, that she sent a letter to him telling him the fact of my suffering. She thinks I am in a very bad state through insufficient food, and, Mr. Holmes, it is true! for no one but God and myself really know how I have existed. I rarely know what it is to get a proper meal, for often I do not expend a sixpence on food in a week when I pay my way, and thank God I have been able to do this up to the present somehow or other; but all my treasures are gone, and I look round and wonder what next!

"My eyes rest on my dear old violin, which is a memory of the past, although long silent. It has been a great grief to me the parting with one thing after another, but I go on hoping for better days that I may regain them; alas! many are now beyond recall.

"The parish doctor has been suggested again, but I feel I would rather die than submit, after all this long struggle and holding out, especially, as I have been able to keep things a little near the mark; when they get beyond me, rather than debt I must give in!

"Still, I hope for better days, and trust things will brighten for me and others, for God knows there are many silent sufferers ebbing their lives away, plodding and struggling with life's battle. My heart bleeds for them, yet I am powerless to help them or myself."

Time and space do not avail, or I could tell story after story of such lives, for in the underworld they are numerous enough. Who can wonder that some of them "are made bitter by misfortune"? Who can wonder that others "are driven to wrong"? Who can be surprised that "many drift into lives of hopeless uselessness"? Surely our friend knew what she was talking about, in the underworld though she be. She sees that there are deeps below the depths, that she herself is in. Though ill, starving and hopeless about her own future, she is troubled for others, for she adds, "since I have known the horror of this life, my heart goes out to others that are enduring it."

Now this class of woman is not much in evidence till the final catastrophe comes, when the doors of a one-roomed home are closed against them. Even then they do not obtrude themselves on our observation, for they hide themselves away till the river or canal gives up its dead.

But it is not every woman that maintains such a high tone, for once in the underworld the difficulty of personal cleanliness confronts them, and dirt kills self-respect. Poverty makes them acquainted with both physical and moral dirt, and the effect of one night in a shelter or lodging-house is often sufficient to destroy self-respect and personal cleanliness for life.

I am quite sure that I am voicing the opinion of all who have knowledge of the underworld in which such women are compelled to live, when I say that the great want in London and in all our large towns is suitable and well-managed lodging-houses under municipal control and inspection, where absolute cleanliness and decency can be assured. Lodging-houses to which women in their hour of sore need may turn with the certainty that their self-respect will not be destroyed. But under the present conditions decent women have no chance of retaining their decency or recovering their standing in social life.

Listen again! a widowed tooth-brush maker speaks to us: "Dear Mr. Holmes, I feel that I must thank you for still allowing me a pension, and I do thank you so much in increasing it. When I received it my heart was so full of joy that I could not speak. My little boys are growing, and they require more than when my husband died six years ago. I am sure it has been a great struggle, but I have found such a great help in you, I do not know how to thank you for all that you have done for me and many poor workers.

"I do hope that God will still give you health and strength to carry on the good work which you are doing for us. When I last spoke to you I thought my little boys were much better, but I am sorry to say that when I took them to Great Ormond Street Hospital, they said they were both suffering from heart disease, and I was to keep them from school for a time; and they also suffer from rheumatics. They are to get out all they can. I have been taking them to the hospital for over two years, and sometimes I feel downhearted, as I had hoped they would have improved before this.

"The eldest boy does not have fits now, and this I am thankful for. But I feel that I am wasting a lot of your time reading this letter, so I must thank you very much for all your great goodness to me."

But one of the boys is now dead, to the other "fits" have returned, and the widow still sits, sits and sits at her tooth-brushes in poverty and hunger.

Listen to an old maid's story; she is a shoe machinist: "Yes, sir, I have kept them for six years, and I hope to keep them till they can keep themselves, and then perhaps they will help to keep me."

The speaker was a worn and feeble woman of fifty-five years, at least that was the age she gave me, and most certainly she did not look less. We were talking about her two boys, her nephews, whose respective ages were eleven and thirteen.

"Both their parents died six years ago; their father was my only brother, and their mother had neither brothers nor sisters! Of course I took them; what else could I do? What! Send them to the workhouse? Not while I can work for them. Ah, sir! you were only joking!" In this she was partly right, for I had merely offered the suggestion in order to draw her out.

"So after the double funeral they came to live with you?" "Yes." "Did their parents leave any money?" "Money, no! How can poor people leave any money? their club money paid for the funeral and the doctor's bill." "So they owed nothing?" "Not a penny; if they had, I should have paid it somehow."

And doubtless she would, though how, it passes my wit to conceive. But there, it would have meant only a few more hours' work daily for the brave old spinster, but not for the boys, for they would have been fed while she fasted, they would have slept while she worked.

"Yes," she continued, "I am a boot machinist, and it is pretty hard work; we had a tough time when I had to pay two shillings weekly for that machine, but we managed, and now you see it is paid for, it is my own; but really, times are harder for us. The boys are growing and want more food and clothing; they go to school, and must have boots; it's the boots that floor me, they cost a lot of money."

I called the boys to me and examined their boots; their old aunt looked as if she was going to prevent me, but presently she said, "I had no work last week, or I should have got him a pair." "Him" was the younger boy, whose boots, or the remains of them, presented a deplorable appearance; and, truth to tell, the elder boy's were not much better. So I said to the brave old soul, "Look here, I will give these boys a good new pair of boots each on one condition!" "What is that." "That you allow me to buy you a pair." Again there was a look of resentment, but I continued, "I am quite sure that you require boots as badly as your boys, and I cannot think of them having nice boots and you going without, so I want you to all start equal; kindly put out your foot and let me look." In a shamefaced sort of a way she put her left foot forward; a strange, misshapen, dilapidated apology of a boot covered the left foot. "Now the right," I said. "Never mind looking at the other, it does not matter, does it?" she said. "Yes, it does," so the right foot was presented; one glance was enough! "That will do; come along for three pairs of boots."

They returned home, the boys rejoicing in their new boots, and their feeble old aunt tolerating hers for the sake of her boys. Dear, brave, self-denying, indomitable old maid. She had visited the fatherless in their afflictions, she had toiled unceasingly for six long years, she had taken willingly upon her weak shoulders a heavy burden; a burden that, alas! many strong men are only too willing to cast upon others. She had well earned her pair of boots, and sincerely do I hope that when her poor feet get accustomed to their circumscribed area, and the pressure of well-made boots has become comforting, that she will derive pleasure from them, even though they represent "the first charity that I have ever received."

But is it not wonderful, this marvellous self-denial of the very poor! Other spheres of life doubtless produce many noble lives and heroic characters, but was ever a braver deed done than this feeble and weary old maid did?

And it was all so natural, so commonplace, so very matter-of-fact, for when I spoke warmly of her deed she said very simply, "Well, what else could I do!"

And in the underworld, amidst the dirt and squalor, the poverty, the high rents, and the poor, poor earnings of poor, poor women, there are plenty like her.

God grant that when the lads can work they will lighten her burdens and cheer her heart by working for her who had worked so hard for them.

Listen also to the story of the blouse-makers disclosed to the upper world by the Press.

"A pathetic story of poverty was told to the Hackney coroner, who held an inquiry into the death of Emily Langes, 59, a blouse-maker of Graham Road, Dalston. Death was due to starvation.

"Annie Marie, an aged sister, said they had both been in great poverty for a very long time. They had worked at blouse-making as long as they could, but that work had fallen off so much that really all they had got to live on was by selling off their home.

They had not enough to live on, and had to pay four shillings and sixpence rent.

"The coroner: 'Selling your home will soon come to an end. You had best apply in the proper direction for help; the parish must bury her. Don't go on ruining yourself by selling off things.'

"Mr. Ingham, relieving officer for the No. 7 ward at Hackney, said that he knew the old couple. He remembered giving relief to both sisters about two months ago, but had had no application since. He offered the 'House' to the living sister.

"A juror: 'Are questions put which might upset a proud respectable old couple when they ask for relief?'

"Witness: 'Of course we have to inquire into their means pretty closely.'

"The coroner: 'It seems pretty clear that the old couple were too proud to ask for help.'

"The jury returned a verdict that Emily Langes died from exhaustion caused by want of food."

But listen again! as we stand in the land of crushed womanhood and starving childhood. We hear a gentle voice, "Mother, it is nearly one o'clock, the men have gone by from the public-house; you go to bed, dear, and I will finish the work." A feeble woman, with every nerve broken, rises from her machine, shakes her dress and lies down on her bed, but her daughter sits on and on.

Oh the sighs and groans and accents of sorrow that come upon our listening ears! Oh the weariness, the utter weariness of this land below the line!

Midnight! and thousands of women are working! One o'clock, and thousands are still at it! Two o'clock, the widows are still at work! Thank God the children are asleep. Three o'clock a.m., the machines cease to rattle, and in the land of crushed womanhood there is silence if not peace. But who is to pay? Shall we ultimately evolve a people that require no sleep, that cannot sleep if they would? Is crushed womanhood to produce human automatic machines? Or is civilisation generally to pay the penalty for all this grinding of human flesh and blood? Let me tell the story of an old machinist! I have told part of it before, but the sequel must be told. I had made the acquaintance and friendship of three old women in Bethnal Green who lived together, and collaborated in their work. They made trousers for export trade; one machined, one finished, and one pressed, brave old women all! They all worked in the machinist's room, for this saved gas and coal, and prevented loss of time. At night they separated, each going to her own room. The machinist was a widow, and her machine had been bought out of her husband's club and insurance money when he died twenty-one years before. I had often seen it, heard its rattle, and witnessed its whims.

She once told me that it required a new shuttle, and I offered to pay for one; but she said, "I cannot part with it; it will last my time, for I want a new shuttle too!"

Six months after she was found dead in her bed by her partners when they came to resume work.

Her words had come true! The old machine stood silent under the little window; its old shuttle no longer whirred and rattled with uncertain movements. It was motionless and cold. On a little bed the poor old brave woman lay cold and motionless too! for the shuttle of her life had stopped, never to move again.

The heroic partnership of the old women was broken, never in this world to be resumed, and so two old hearts sorrowed and two troubled minds wondered how they would be able to live without her.

I knew her well; it was my privilege to give her some happiness and some change from grime and gloom, to take her away sometimes from

the wayward shuttle and rattling machine. I knew that she would
have selected such a death could she have chosen, for she dreaded the
parish. I think, too, that she would have wished for her old machine
to be buried with her, and for its silent shuttle to be beside her in her
coffin. To her it was a companion, and for it her husband died.
Twenty-one years the machine and herself had lived with each other
and for each other. Sharing with each other's toil, if not each other's
hopes and fears! Working! working! unceasingly through life—in
death and rest they were not divided.

It was a blessed thing that her machine partner required no food,
or life would have been even more serious than it was. But it had its
whims and its moods, sometimes it resented everlasting work at three-
half-pence per hour for the pair of them, and it "jibbed." But a little
oil and a soothing word, and, it must be feared, sometimes with a
threat, and the old thing went again.

Surely it will be sacrilege for any one else to sit upon that old chair
and try to renew the life and motion of the old machine!

It is strange that this oppression of women which is the cause of
my greatest sorrow should also be the cause of my keenest joy. But it
is so! And why? Because I number two thousand of these underworld
women slaves among my personal friends, and I am proud of it! The
letters I have given are a few out of hundreds that I have received. I
know these women as few know them. I know their sufferings and
their virtues, their great content and their little requirements. I know
that they have the same capabilities for happiness as other people, and
I know that they get precious little chance of exercising those capabilities. Strange again, I get no begging letters from them, though I
do from others who are better placed. I declare it to be wonderful!
This endurance and patience of London's miserably paid women. I
tell you that I am the happiest man alive! Why? Because during
the present year a thousand of my poor friends from the under
world came up for a time and had a fortnight, a whole fortnight's rest
each with food and comfort in a beautiful rest home by the sea.

For kind friends have enabled me to build one for them and for them alone!

And I was there sometimes to see, and it was good for me. So Mrs. Holmes and myself make frequent visits to the rest home, and every time we visit it we become more and more convinced that not only is it a "Palace Beautiful," but that it is also a joy to the slave women who have the good fortune to spend a holiday (all too short) in it.

Gloom cannot enter "Singholm" or, if it does enter, it promptly and absolutely disappears. Ill-temper cannot live there, the very flowers smile it away. The atmosphere itself acts like "laughing gas." So the house fairly rings with merry laughter from elderly staid women equally as from the younger ones, whose contact with serious and saddening life has not been so paralysing to joyous emotions.

It did us good to hear such jolly laughter from throats and organs that, but for Singholm, must have rusted and decayed.

One of our trustees was with us, it being his first visit to the home. I know that he was surprised at the size, the beauty, the comfort and refinement of the whole place. The garden filled him with delight, the skill of the architect in planning the building, together with the style, gave him increased pleasure.

The great drawing-room and the equally large dining-room rather astonished him. The little bedrooms he declared perfect. But what astonished him most of all was the unaffected happiness of the women; for this I do not think he was prepared. Well, as I have said, gloom cannot live in Singholm, and this I have found out by personal experience, for if I am quite cross and grumpy in London, I cannot resist the exhilaration that prevails at Singholm among London's underworld women.

I think I may say that our trustee was surprised at something else! But then he is a bachelor, and so of course does not understand the infinite resources of femininity.

"How nice they look," he said. "How well they dress"; and, once again, "How clean and tidy they are; how well their colours blend!"

Thank God for this! we hold no truce with dirt at Singholm; we bid dowdyism begone! avaunt! I will tell you a secret! Singholm demands respect for itself and self-respect for its inmates.

Our trustee's testimony is true; the women belonging to our association do look nice; when they are at Walton they rise to the occasion as if they were to the manner born.

When, with their cheap white or blue blouses, they sit under the palms in our drawing-room, all, even the oldest and poorest, neat—nay, smart if you will—they present a picture that can only be appreciated by those who know their lives. Some people might find fault, but to me the colour and tone of the picture is perfect.

As there were seventy of them, there was room for variety, and they gave it! Look at them! There they sit as the shades of night are falling. They have been out all day long, and have come in tired. Are they peevish? Not a bit! Are they downhearted? No!

There is my friend who makes no secret about it, and tells us that she is forty-six years of age; this is the first time she has ever seen the sea, and she laughs at the thought. The sun has browned, reddened and roughened her face, and when I say, "How delicate you look," she bursts again into merry laughter, and the whole party join her. Mrs. Holmes and myself join in, and our worthy trustee, bachelor and Quaker though he be, laughs merriest of all.

Aye! but this laughter was sweet music, but somehow it brought tears to my eyes.

Now just look at my friend over there beside one of the palms, her feet resting so naturally on the Turkey carpet! You observe she sits majestically in a commodious chair; she needs one! For she is five feet eleven inches in height, and weighs sixteen stone. I call her "The Queen," for when she stands up she is erect and queenly with a noble head and pleasing countenance.

She makes no secret about her age; "I am sixty, and I have been here four times, and, please God, I'll come forty-four more times," and she looks like it. But what if there had been no Singholm to look forward to year by year? Why, then she would have been heavy in heart as well as in body, and her erect form would have been bent, for she is a hard worker from Bethnal Green.

The idea of coming forty-four more times to Singholm, and she sixty-six, was the signal for more laughter, and again Singholm was tested; but our builder had done his work well.

"Turn on the electric light, matron!" There is a transformation scene for you! Now you see the delicate art colours in the Turkey carpets, and the subdued colours in the Medici Society's reproduced pictures.

See how they have ranged their chairs all round by the walls, and the centre of the room is unoccupied, saving here and there maiden-hair ferns and growing flowers. Now look at the picture in its fulness! and we see poor old bent and feeble bodies bowed with toil, and faces furrowed by unceasing anxiety; but the sun, the east wind, the sea air and Singholm have brightened and browned them.

There is my poor old friend, long past threescore and ten, to whom Singholm for a time is verily Heaven; but—"Turn on the gramophone, please, matron." Thanks to a kind friend, we have a really good one, with a plentiful supply of records. The matron, in the wickedness of her heart, turns on an orchestral "cakewalk." The band plays, old bodies begin to move and sway, and seventy pair of feet begin unconsciously to beat the floor. Laughter again resounds; our Quaker himself enters into the spirit of it, so I invite him to lead off with the "Queen" for his partner, at which he was dismayed, although he is a veritable son of Anak.

But to my dismay the bent and feeble septuagenarian offered to lead off with myself as partner, at which I collapsed, for alas, I cannot dance. Then our trustee led the roars of laughter that testified to my discomfiture.

So we had no dancing, only a cakewalk. But we had more merriment and music, and then our little evening service. "What hymn shall we have?" Many voices called out, "Sun of my soul," so the matron went to the piano, and I listened while they sang "Watch by the sick, enrich the poor," which for me, whenever the poor, the feeble and aged sing it, has a power and a meaning that I never realise when the organ leads a well-trained choir and a respectable church congregation to blend their voices.

Then I read to them a few words from the old, but ever new, Book, and closed with a few simple, well-known prayers, and then—as old Pepys has it—"to bed."

We watch them file up the great staircase one by one, watch them disappear into their sweet little rooms and clean sheets. To me, at any rate, the picture was more comforting and suggestive than Burne Jones's "Golden Stairs." In fifteen minutes the electric light was switched off, and Singholm was in darkness and in peace. But outside the stars were shining, the flowers still blooming, the garden was full of the mystery of sweet odours; close by the sea was singing its soothing lullaby, and God was over all!

But let us get back to the underworld!

"How long have we lived together, did you ask? well, ever since we were born, and she is sixty-seven," pointing to a paralysed woman, who was sitting in front of the window. "I am two years younger," she continued, "and we have never been separated; we have lived together, worked together, and slept together, and if ever we did have a holiday, we spent it together. And now we are getting old, just think of it! I am sixty-five, isn't it terrible? They always used to call us 'the girls' when mother, father and my brothers were alive, but they have all gone—not one of them left. But we 'girls' are left, and now we are getting old—sixty-five—isn't it terrible? We ought to be ashamed of it, I suppose, but we are not, are we, dear? For we are just 'the girls' to each other, and sometimes I feel as strong and as young as a girl."

"How long have you lived in the top of this four-storey house?" I asked. "Sixteen years," came the reply. "All alone?" "No, sir, we have been together." "And your sister, how long has she been paralysed?" "Before we came to this house." "Does she ever go out?" "Of course she does; don't I take her out in the bath-chair behind you?" "Can she wash and dress herself, do her hair, and make herself as clean and tidy as she is?" "I do it for her."

"But how do you get her down these interminable stairs?" I asked.

"She does that herself, sitting down and going from step to step," she said, and then added, "but it is hard work for her, and it takes her a very long time."

"Now tell me," I said, "have you ever had a holiday?" "Yes, we have had one since my sister became paralysed, and we went to Herne Bay." "Did you take the bath-chair with you?" "Of course we did; how could she go without it?" "And you pushed her about Herne Bay, and took her on the sands in it?" I said. "Of course," she said quite naturally, as if she was surprised at my question. "Now tell me how much rent do you pay for these two rooms?" "Seven shillings and sixpence per week; I know it is too much, but I must have a good window for her, where she can sit and look out." "How do you do your washing?" "I pay the landlady a shilling a week to do it." "How long have you worked at umbrella covering?" "Ever since we left school, both of us; we have never done anything else." "How long have your parents been dead" "More than forty years," was the answer.

To every one of the replies made by the younger sister, the paralytic at the window nodded her head in confirmation as though she would say, "Quite true, quite true!"

"Forgive me asking so many questions, but I want to understand how you live; you pay seven-and-six rent, and one shilling for washing every week; that comes to eight shillings and sixpence before you buy food, coal, and pay for gas; and you must burn a lot of gas, for I am sure that you work till a very late hour," and the elder sister nodded her head. "Yes, gas is a big item, but I manage it," and then the elder one spoke. "Yes, she is a wonderful manager! a wonderful manager! she is better than I ever was." "Well, dear, you managed well, you know you did, and we saved some money then, didn't we!"

"Ah! we did, but mine is all gone, and I can't work now; but you are a good manager, better than I ever was."

I looked at the aged and brave couple, and took stock of their old but still good furniture that told its own story, and said, "You had two accounts in the Post-Office Savings Bank, and when you both worked you saved all you could?" "Yes, sir, we worked hard, and never wasted anything." Again the sixty-seven old girl broke in: "But mine is all gone, all gone, but she is a wonderful manager." "And mine is nearly all gone, too," said the younger, "but I can work for both of us," and the elder sister nodded her head as if she would say, "And she can, too!" I looked at the dozen umbrellas before me, and said, "What do you get for covering these?" "Ah! that's what's called, vulgarly speaking, a bit of jam! they are gents' best umbrellas, and I shall get three shillings for them. I got them out yesterday from the ware-house, after waiting there for two hours. I shall work till twelve to-night and finish them by midday to-morrow; they are my very best work." Three shillings for a dozen! her very best work! and she finding machine and thread, and waiting two hours at the factory!

"Come," I said, "tell me what you earned last week, and how many hours you worked?" "I earned ten shillings and sixpence; but don't ask me how many hours I worked, for I don't know; I begin when it is light, because that saves gas, and I work as long as I can, for I am strong and have good health." "But," I said, "you paid eight shillings and sixpence for rent and washing; that left you with two shillings. Does your sister have anything from the parish?" I felt sorry that I had put the question, for I got a proud "No, sir," followed by some tears from the sixty-five-year-old "girl." Presently I said, "However do you spend it?" "Didn't I tell you that I had saved some, and was drawing it? But I manage, and get a bit of meat, too!" Again from the window came the words, "She is a good manager."

"What will you do when you have drawn all your savings?" "Oh! I shall manage, and God is good," was all I could get.

A brave, heroic soul, surely, dwells in that aged girl, for in her I found no bitterness, no repining; nay, I found a sense of humour and the capability of a hearty laugh as we talked on and on, for I was in wonderland.

When I rose to leave, she offered to accompany us—for a friend was with me—downstairs to the door; I said, "No, don't come down, we will find our way; stop and earn half-a-crown, and please remember that you are sixty-five." "Hush!" she said, "the landlady will hear you; don't tell anybody, isn't it awful? and we were called the girls," and she burst into a merry laugh. During our conversation the paralysed sister had several times assured me that she "would like to have a ride in a motor-car." This I am afraid I cannot promise her, much as I would like to do so; but the exact object of my visit was to make arrangements for "the girls" to go to our home of rest for a whole fortnight.

And they went, bath-chair as well. For sixteen long years they had not seen the sea or listened to its mighty voice, but for a whole fortnight they enjoyed its never-ending wonder and inhaled its glorious breath. And the younger "girl" pushed the chair, and the older "girl" sat in it the while they prattled, and talked and managed, till almost the days of their real girlhood came back to them. Dull penury and sordid care were banished for a whole fortnight and appetite came by eating. The older "girl" said, "If I stop here much longer, I know I shall walk," and she nearly managed it too, for when helped out of her chair, she first began to stand, and then to progress a little step by step by holding on to any friendly solid till she almost became a child again. But the fortnight ended all too soon, and back to their upper room, the window and the umbrellas they came, to live that fortnight over and over again, and to count the days, weeks and months that are to elapse before once again the two old girls and an old—so old— bath-chair will revel and joy, eat and rest, prattle and laugh by the sea.

But they have had their "motor ride," too! and the girls sat side by side, and although it was winter time they enjoyed it, and they have a new theme for prattle.

I have since ascertained that the sum of ten shillings, and ten shillings only, remained in the Post-Office Savings Bank to the credit of the managing sister.

But I have also learned something else quite as pitiful—it is this: the allowance of coal during the winter months for these heroic souls was one half-hundredweight per week, fifty-six lb., which cost them eightpence-halfpenny.

VIII

Marriage in the Underworld

Young folk marry and are given in marriage at a very early age in the underworld. Their own personal poverty and thousands of warning examples are not sufficient to deter them. Strange to say, their own parents encourage them, and, more strange still, upperworld people of education and experience lend a willing hand in what is at the best a deplorable business.

Under their conditions it is perhaps difficult to say what other course can or ought to be taken, for their homes are like beehives, and "swarming" time inevitably comes. That oftentimes comes when young people of either sex are midway in their "teens." The cramped little rooms or room that barely sufficed for the parents and small children are altogether out of the question when the children become adolescent. The income of the family is not sufficient to allow the parents, even if they were desirous of doing so, taking larger premises with an extra bedroom. Very few parents brace themselves to this endeavour, for it means not only effort but expense. So the young folks swarm either to lodgings, or to marriage, and the pretence of home life.

Private lodgings for girls are dangerous and expensive, while public lodgings for youths are probably a shade worse. So marriage it is, and boys of nineteen unite with girls one or two years younger.

I have no doubt that the future looks very rosy to the young couple whose united earnings may amount to as much as thirty shillings weekly, for it is an axiom of the poor that two can live cheaper than one.

It is so easy to pay a deposit on a single room, and so easy, so very easy, to purchase furniture on the hire system. Does not the youth give his mother ten shillings weekly? Why not give it to a wife? Does not the girl contribute to her mother's exchequer? Why may not she become a wife and spend her own earnings? Both are heartily sick of their present home life, any change must be for the better! So marriage it is! But they have saved nothing, they are practically penniless beyond the current week's wages. Never mind, they can get their wedding outfit on the pay weekly rule, the parson will marry them for nothing. "Here's a church, let's go in and get married." Christmas, Easter or Bank Holiday comes to their aid, and they do it! and, heigho! for life's romance.

The happy bride continues at the factory, and brings her shillings to make up the thirty. They pay three shillings and sixpence weekly for their room, one-and-six weekly for their household goods, two more shillings weekly are required for their wedding clothes, that is all! Have they not twenty-three shillings left!

They knew that they could manage it! All goes merrily as a marriage bell! Hurrah! They can afford a night or two a week at a music-hall; why did they not get married before? how stupid they had been!

But something happens, for the bride becomes a mother. Her wages cease, and thirty shillings weekly for two is a very different matter to twenty shillings for three!

They had to engage an old woman for nurse for one week only. But that cost seven shillings and sixpence. A number of other extras are incurred, all to be paid out of his earnings. They have not completed the hire purchase business; they have even added to that expense by the purchase of a bassinet at one shilling weekly for thirty weeks. The bassinet, however, serves one useful purpose, it saves the expense of a cradle.

In less than a fortnight the girl mother is again knocking at the factory door. She wishes to become an "out-worker"; the manager, knowing her to be a capable machinist, gives her work, and promises her a constant supply.

Now they are all right again! Are they? Why, she has no sewing-machine! Stranded again! not a bit of it. The hire purchase again comes to her help. Eighteenpence deposit is paid, a like weekly payment promised, signed for and attended to; and lo! a sparkling new sewing-machine is deposited in their one room. Let us take an inventory of their goods: one iron bedstead, flock mattress, two pairs of sheets, two blankets and a common counterpane, a deal chest of drawers, a deal table, two Windsor chairs, a bassinet carriage, a sewing-machine, fire-shovel, fender and poker, some few crocks, a looking-glass, a mouth-organ and a couple of towels, some knives, forks and spoons, a tea-pot, tea-kettle, saucepan and frying-pan. But I have been very liberal! They stand close together, do those household goods; they crowd each other, and if one moves, it jostles the other. The sewing-machine stands in front of the little window, for it demands the light. It took some scheming to arrange this, but husband and wife ultimately managed it. The bassinet stands close to the machine, that the girl mother may push it gently when baby is cross, and that she may reach the "soother" and replace it when it falls from baby's mouth.

Now she is settled down! off she goes! She starts on a life of toil, compared to which slavery is light and pleasant. Oh, the romance of it; work from morn till late at night. The babe practically unwashed, the house becomes grimy, and the bed and bassinet nasty. The husband's wages have not risen, though his expenses have; other children come and some go; they get behind with their rent; an "ejectment order" is enforced. The wretched refuse of the home is put on the street pavement, the door is locked against them, and the wretched couple with their children are on the pavement too! The only thing to survive the wreck is the sewing-machine. The only thing that I know among the many things supplied to the poor on the hire system that is the least bit likely to stand the wear and tear is the machine. Doubtless the poor pay highly for it; still it is comforting to know that in this one direction the poor are supplied with good articles. And the poor respect their machines, as the poor always respect things that are not shoddy.

I have drawn no fancy picture, but one that holds true with regard to thousands. Evils that I cannot enumerate and that imagination cannot exaggerate wait upon and attend these unfortunate, nay, criminal marriages; which very largely are the result of that one great all-pervading cause—the housing of the poor.

But in the underworld there are much worse kinds of married life than the one I have pictured, for those young people did start life with some income and some hopes. But what can be said about, and what new condemnation can be passed upon, the marriage of feeble-minded, feeble-bodied, homeless wanderers? United in the bonds of holy matrimony by an eager clergy, and approved in this deplorable step by an all-wise State, thousands of crazy, curious, wretched, penniless individuals, to whom even the hire system is impossible, join their hopeless lives.

Half idiots of both sexes in our workhouses look at each other, and then take their discharge after a mutual understanding. They experience no difficulty in finding clergymen ready to marry them and unite them in the bonds of poverty and the gall of wretchedness. The blessing of the Church is pronounced upon this coupling, and away they go!

Over their lives and means of living I will draw a veil, for common decency forbids me to speak, as common decency ought to have forbidden their marriage.

But down in the underworld, and very low down, too, are numberless couples whose plight is perhaps worse, for they have at any rate known the refined comfort of good homes, but remembrance only adds poignancy to suffering and despair.

Read the following story, and after condemnation upon condemnation has been passed upon the thoughtless or wicked marriages of the poor, tell me, if you will, what condemnation shall be passed upon the educated when they, through marriage, drag down into this inferno innocent, loving and pure women?

It was Boxing Day in a London police-court. Twenty-five years have passed, but that day is as fresh in my memory as though it were yesterday. The prisoners' rooms were filled, the precincts of the court were full, and a great crowd of witnesses and friends, or of the curious public, were congregated in the street.

Yesterday had been the great Christian festival, the celebration of the birth of the Prince of Peace, when the bells had rang out the old story "Peace on earth, good-will to men." To-day it looked as though Hell had been holding carnival!

Nearly one hundred prisoners had to come before the magistrate. I can see them now! as one by one they passed before him, for time has not dimmed the vivid picture of that procession. I remember their stories, and think still of their cuts and wounds. Outside the court the day was dull, and inside the light was bad and the air heavy with the fumes of stale debauch and chloride of lime. And yesterday had been Christmas Day in the metropolis of Christendom.

Hours passed, and the kindly magistrate sat on apportioning punishment, fitting the sentence as it were by instinct. At two o'clock he rose for a short recess, a hasty luncheon, and then back to his task.

At the end of the long procession came a smitten woman. Darkness and fog now enveloped the court as the woman stood in the dock. Her age was given as twenty-eight; her occupation pickle-making. First let me picture that woman and then tell her story, for she represents a number of women into whose forlorn faces I have looked and of whose hopeless hearts I have an intimate knowledge.

Some men have conquered evil habits, helped by the love of a pure woman, without which they would have vainly struggled or have readily succumbed. But while I know this, I think of the women who have fastened the tendrils of their heart's affection round unworthy men, and have married them, hoping, trusting and believing that their love and influence would be powerful enough to win the men to sobriety and virtue. Alas! how mistaken they have been! What they have endured! Of such was this woman! There she stood, the embodiment of woe. A tall, refined woman, her clothing poor and sparse, her head enveloped in surgical bandages.

In the darkness of the Christmas night she had leaped from the wall of a canal bridge into the murky gloom, her head had struck the bank, and she rolled into the thick, black water.

It was near the basin of the Surrey Canal, and a watchman on duty had pulled her out; she had been taken to a hospital and attended to. Late in the afternoon the policeman brought her to the court, where a charge of attempted suicide was brought against her. But little evidence was taken, and the magistrate ordered a week's remand. In the cells I had a few moments' conversation with her, but all I could get from her was the pitiful moan, "Why didn't they let me die? why didn't they let me die?"

In a week's time I saw her again; surgical bandages were gone, medical attention and a week's food and rest had done something for her, but still she was the personification of misery.

I offered to take charge of her, and as she quietly promised not to repeat the attempt, the magistrate kindly committed her to my care. So we went to her room: it was a poor place, and many steps we climbed before we entered it. High up as the room was, and small as were its dimensions, she, out of the nine shillings she earned at the pickle factory paid three and sixpence weekly for it. I had gathered from what she had told me that she was in poverty and distress. So on our way I brought a few provisions; leaving these and a little money with her, I left her promising to see her again after a few days. But before leaving she briefly told me her story, a sad, sad story, but a story to be read and pondered.

She was the only daughter of a City merchant, and had one brother. While she was quite a child her mother died, and at an early age she managed her father's household. She made the acquaintance of a clever and accomplished man who was an accountant. He was older than she, and of dissipated habits. Her father had introduced him to his home and daughter, little thinking of the consequences that ensued. She had no mother to guide her, she was often lonely, for her father was immersed in his business.

In a very short time she had fixed her heart on to the man, and when too late her father expostulated, and finally forbade the man the house. This only intensified her love and led to quarrels with her father. Ultimately they married, and had a good home and two servants. In a little over three years two children added to her joys and sorrows. Still her husband's faults were not amended, but his dissipation increased. Monetary difficulties followed, and to avoid disgrace her father was called upon to provide a large sum of money.

This did not add to his sympathy, but it estranged the father and child.

Then difficulties followed, and soon her husband stood in the dock charged with embezzlement. Eighteen months' imprisonment was awarded him, but the greater punishment fell upon the suffering wife. Her father refused to see her, so with her two little ones she was left to face the future. Parting with most of her furniture, jewellery, servant, she gave up her house, took two small rooms, and waited wearily for the eighteen months to pass.

They passed, and her husband came back to her. But his character was gone, the difficulty of finding employment stared him in the face.

He joined the ranks of the shabby-genteel to live somehow by bits of honest work, mixed with a great deal of dishonest work. Four years of this life, two more children for the mother, increasing drunkenness, degenerating into brutality on her husband's part. Her father's death and some little money left to her gave momentary respite. But the money soon went. Her brother had taken the greater portion and had gone into a far country. This was the condition of affairs when her husband was again arrested; this time for forgery. There was no doubt about his guilt, and a sentence of five years' penal servitude followed. Again she parted with most of her home, reducing it to one room.

With her four children round her she tried to eke out an existence. She soon became penniless, and ultimately with her children took refuge in a London workhouse. After a time the guardians sent the four children to their country school and nursing home, when she was free to leave the workhouse and get her own living.

She came out with a letter of introduction to the pickle factory, and obtained employment at nine shillings a week. The weeks and months passed, her daily task and common round being a mile walk to the factory, ten hours' work, and then the return journey. One week-end on her homeward journey she was attracted and excited by a fire; when she resumed her journey she was penniless, her week's wages had been stolen from her. Her only warm jacket and decent pair of boots then had to be pawned, for the rent must be paid. Monday found her again at the monotonous round, but with added hardships.

She missed the jacket and the boots, and deprived herself of food that she might save enough money wherewith to take them out of pawn. Christmas Eve came, and she had not recovered them. She sat in her room lonely and with a sad heart, but there was mirth and noise below her, for even among the poor Bacchus must be worshipped at Christmas time.

One of the women thought of the poor lone creature up at the top of the house, and fetched her down. They had their bottles of cheap spirits, for which they had paid into the publican's Christmas club. She drank, and forgot her misery. Next morning, when the bells of a neighbouring church were ringing out, they awoke her as she lay fully dressed on her little bed. She felt ill and dazed, and by and by the consciousness came to her of last night's drinking. Christmas Day she spent alone, ill, miserable and ashamed. "I must have been drunk!" she kept repeating to herself, and on Christmas night she sought her death.

I wrote to kind friends, and interested some ladies in her welfare. Plenty of clothing was sent for her; a better room, not quite so near the sky, was procured for her. Her daily walk to the factory was stopped, for more profitable work was given to her. Finally I left her in the hands of kind friends that I knew would care for her.

Two years passed, and on Christmas Eve I called with a present and a note sent her by a friend. She was gone—her husband had been released on ticket-of-leave, had found her and joined her, and for a time she kept him as well as herself. He was more brutal than before, and in his fury, either drunk or sober, he frequently beat her, so that the people of the house had to send them away. Where they had moved to, I failed to find out, but they had vanished!

Fourteen months passed, and one bitterly cold day in February at the end of a long row of prisoners, waiting their turn to appear before the magistrate, stood the woman wretched and ill, with a puling bit of mortality in her arms.

She was a "day charge," having been arrested for stealing a pot of condensed milk. At length she stood before the magistrate, and the evidence was given that she was seen to take the milk and hurry away. She was arrested with the milk on her.

It was believed that she had taken milk from the same place at other times. When asked what she had to say in extenuation, she held her child up and said, "I did not take it for myself, I took it for this!" She did not call it her child. The magistrate looked, shuddered, and sentenced her to one day.

So once again I stood face to face with her, and face to face with a big man who had been waiting for her, who insolently asked me what I wanted with his wife. I turned from him to the woman, and asked if she would leave him, for if so I would provide for her.

Mournfully she shook her head; leave him, no!—to the bitter end she stood by him.

So they passed from my view, the educated brute and the despairing, battered, faithful drudge of a woman, to migrate from lodging-house to lodging-house, to suffer and to die!

If all the girls of England could see what I have seen, if they could take, as I have taken, some measure of the keen anguish and sorrow that comes from such a step, they would never try the dangerous experiment of marrying a man in the hope of reforming him. Should, perchance, young women read this story, let me tell them it is true in every particular, but not the whole truth, for there are some things that cannot be told.

Again and again I have heard poor stricken women cry: "How can you! how can you!" More than once my manhood has been roused, and I have struck a blow in their defence.

If there is one piece of advice that, in the light of my experience, I would like to burn into the very consciousness of young women, it is this: if they have fastened their heart's love about a man, and find that thorough respect does not go with that love, then, at whatever cost, let them crush that love as they would crush a serpent's egg.

And the same holds good with men: I have known men in moments of passion marry young women, trusting that a good home and an assured income would restore them to decency and womanhood—but in vain! I saw a foul-looking woman far from old sent again to prison, where she had been more than a hundred times. She had also served two years in an inebriate reformatory. Fifteen years ago, when I first met her, she was a fair-looking young woman. Needless to say, I met her in the police-court. A short time afterwards she came to tell me that she was married. She had a good home, her husband was in good circumstances, and knew of her life. A few years of home life, two little children to call her mother; then back to her sensual ways. Prisons, rescue homes, workhouses, inebriate reformatories, all have failed to reclaim her, and she lives to spread moral corruption.

IX

Brains in the Underworld

I hope that, in some of my chapters, I have made it clear that a large proportion of the underworld people are industrious and persevering. I want in this chapter to show that many of them have also ability and brains, gifts and graces. This is a pleasant theme, and I would revel in it, but for the sorrowful side of it.

It may seem strange that people living under their conditions should possess these qualities, but in reality there is nothing strange about it, for Nature laughs at us, and bestows her gifts upon whom she pleases, though I have no doubt that she works to law and order if we only understood.

But we do not understand, and therefore she appears whimsical and capricious. I rather expect that even when eugenists get their way and the human race is born to order, that Dame Nature, the mother of us all, will not consent to be left out of the reckoning. Be that as it may, it is certain she bestows her personal gifts among the very poor equally with the rich. She is a true socialist, and, like Santa Claus, she visits the homes of the very poor and bestows gifts upon their children.

Some of the most perfect ladies I have ever met have been uneducated women living in poverty and gloom. I do not say the most beautiful, for suffering and poverty are never beautiful. Neither can rings of care beneath the eyes, and countless furrows upon the face be considered beautiful. But, apart from this, I have found many personal graces and the perfection of behaviour among some of the poorest. All this I consider more wonderful than the possession of brains, though of brains they are by no means deficient.

Have you ever noticed how pretty the healthy children of the very poor are? I am not speaking of unhealthy and feeble children, who are all too numerous, but of the healthy; for, strange as it may appear, there are many such, even in the underworld. Where do you find such beautiful curly hair as they possess? in very few places! It is perfect in its freedom, texture, colour and curl. Dame Nature has not forgotten them! Where do you find prettier faces, more sparkling eyes and eager expressions? Nowhere! And though their faces become prematurely old, and their eyes become hard, still Dame Nature had not forgotten them at birth; she, at any rate, had done her best for them.

Search any families, bring out the hundreds of pretty children, and I will bring hundreds of children from below the line that will compare with them in beauty of body, face and hair. But they must be under four years of age! No! no! the children of the upperworld have not a monopoly of Dame Nature's gifts.

And it is so with mental gifts and graces; the poor get a good share of them, but the pity is they get so little chance of exercising them. For many splendid qualities wither from disuse or perish from lack of development. But some survive, as the following stories will prove.

It was a hot day in June, and, in company with a friend who wished to learn something about the lives of the very poor, I was visiting in the worst quarters of East London.

As we moved from house to house, the thick air within, and the dirt within and without were almost too much for us. The box-like rooms, the horrible backyards, the grime of the men, women and children, combined with the filth in the streets and gutters, made us sick and faint. We asked ourselves whether it was possible that anything decent, virtuous or intelligent could live under such conditions?

The "place" was dignified by the name of a street, although in reality it was a blind alley, for a high wall closed one end of it. It was very narrow, and while infants played in the unclean gutters, frowsy women discussed domestic or more exciting matters with women on the opposite side.

They discussed us too as we passed, and audibly commented, though not favourably, on our business. I had visited the street scores of times, and consequently I was well known. Unfortunately my address was also well known, for every little act of kindness that I ventured to do in that street had been followed by a number of letters from jealous non-recipients.

I venture to say that from every house save one I had received begging or unpleasant letters, for jealousy of each other's benefits was a marked characteristic of that unclean street. As we entered the house from which no letter had been received, we heard a woman call to her neighbour, "They are going to see the old shoemaker." She was correct in her surmise, and right glad we were to make the old man's acquaintance; not that he was very old, but then fifty-nine in a London slum may be considered old age. He sat in a Windsor arm-chair in a very small kitchen; a window at his back revealed that abomination of desolation, a Bethnal Green backyard. He sat as he had sat for years, bent and doubled up, for some kind of paralysis had overtaken him.

He had a fine head and a pointed beard, his thin and weak neck seemed hardly able to bear its heavy burden. He was not overclean, and his clothes were, to say the least, shabby. But there he sat, his wife at work to maintain him. We stood, for there was no sitting room for us. Grime, misery and poverty were in evidence.

He told us that his forefathers were Huguenots, who fled from France and settled as silk weavers in Spitalfields. He had been apprenticed to boot-and shoe-making, his particular branch of work having been boots and shoes for actresses and operatic singers. That formerly he had earned good money, but the trade declined as he had grown older, and now for some years he had been crippled and unable to work, and dependent upon his wife, who was a machinist.

There did not seem much room for imagination and poetry in his home and life, but the following conversation took place—

"It is a very hard life for you sitting month after month on that chair, unable to do anything!" "It is hard, I do not know what I should do if I could not think." "Oh, you think, do you well, thinking is hard work." "Not to me, it is my pleasure and occupation." "What do you think about?" "All sorts of things, what I have read mostly." "What have you read" "Everything that I could get hold of, novelists, poetry, history and travel." "What novelist do you like best" The answer came prompt and decisive: "Dickens," "Why?" "He loved the poor, he shows a greater belief in humanity than Thackeray." "How do you prove that?" "Well, take Thackeray's VANITY FAIR, it is clever and satirical, but there is only one good character, and he was a fool; but in Dickens you come across character after character that you can't help loving."

"Which of his books do you like best?" "A TALE OF TWO CITIES." "Why?" "Well, because the French Revolution always appeals to me, and secondly because I think the best bit of writing in all his books is the description of Sydney Carton's ride on the tumbrel to the guillotine." "Have you ever read Carlyle's FRENCH REVOLUTION?" "No" "I will lend it to you." "If you do, I will read it."

"How about poetry, what poets do you like?" "The minor poets of two hundred years ago, Herrick, Churchill, Shenstone and others." "Why do you like them?" "They are so pretty, so easy to understand, you know what they mean; they speak of beauty, and flowers and love, their language is tuneful and sweet." Thus the grimy old shoemaker spoke, but I continued: "What about the present-day poets?" Swift came the reply, "We have got none." This was a staggerer, but I suggested: "What about Kipling?" "Too slangy and Coarse!" "Austin?" "Don't ask me." "What of Wordsworth, Tennyson and Browning?" "Well, Wordsworth is too prosy, you have to read such a lot to get a little; Tennyson is a bit sickly and too sentimental, I mean with washy sentiment; Browning I cannot understand, he is too hard for me."

"Now let us talk: about dramatists; you have read Shakespeare?" "Yes, every play again and again." "Which do you like best?" "I like them all, the historical and the imaginative; I have never seen one acted, but to me King Lear is his masterpiece."

So we left him doubled up in his chair, in his grime and poverty, lighting up his poor one room with great creations, bearing his heavy burdens, never repining, thinking great thoughts and re-enacting great events, for his mind to him was a kingdom.

The next day my friend sent a dozen well-selected books, but the old shoemaker never sought or looked for any assistance.

Only a few doors away we happened on a slum tragedy. We stood in a queer little house of one room up and one down stairs. Let me picture the scene! A widow was seated at her machine sewing white buckskin children's boots. Time, five o'clock in the afternoon; she had sat there for many hours, and would continue to sit till night was far advanced.

Suddenly a girl of twelve burst in and threw herself into her mother's arms, crying, "Oh, mother, mother, I have lost the scholarship! Oh, mother, the French was too hard for me!" To our surprise the mother seemed intensely relieved, and said, "Thank God for that!"

But the girl wept! After a time we inquired, and found that the girl, having passed the seventh standard at an elementary school, had been attending a higher grade school, where she had been entered for a competitive examination at a good class secondary school. If she obtained it, the widow would have been compelled to sign an agreement for the girl to remain at school for at least three years. But the widow was practically starving, although working fourteen hours daily. Verily, the conflict of duties forms the tragedy of everyday life. The widow was saved by the advanced French; poor mother and poor girl!

By and by the girl was comforted as we held the prospective of a bright future before her, and got her to talk of her studies; she recited for us a scene from AS YOU LIKE IT, and also Portia's speech, "The quality of mercy is not strained."

Standing near was a boy of not more than ten years, who looked as if he would like to recite for us, and I asked him what standard he was in. "The sixth, sir." "And do you like English Literature?" He did not answer the question exactly, but said, "I know the 'Deserted Village,' by Oliver Goldsmith."

"Where was the 'Deserted Village'?" "Sweet Auburn was supposed to be in Ireland, but it is thought that some of the scenes are taken from English villages."

"Can you give us the 'Village Schoolmaster'?" And he did, with point and emphasis. "Now for the 'Village Parson.'" His memory did not fail or trip, and the widow sat there machining; so we turned to her for more information, and found that she was a Leicester woman, and her parents Scots; she had been a boot machinist from her youth.

Her husband was a "clicker" from Stafford; he had been dead eight years. She was left with four children. She had another daughter of fourteen who had done brilliantly at school, having obtained many distinctions, and at twelve years had passed her "Oxford Local." This girl had picked up typewriting herself, and as she was good at figures and a splendid writer, she obtained a junior clerk's place in the City at seven shillings and sixpence per week. Every day this girl walked to and from her business, and every day the poor widow managed to find her fourpence that the girl might have a lunch in London City.

I felt interested in this girl, so I wrote asking her to come to lunch with me on a certain day. She came with a book in her hand, one of George Eliot's, one of her many prizes. A fourpenny lunch may be conducive to high thinking, may even lead to an appreciation of great novels: it certainly leaves plenty of time for the improvement of the mind, though it does not do much for nourishing the body. I found her exceedingly interesting and intelligent, with some knowledge of "political economy," well up in advanced arithmetic, and quite capable of discussing the books she had read. Yet the family had been born in an apology of a house, they had graduated in the slums, but not in the gutter. Their widowed mother had worked interminable hours and starved as she worked, but no attendance officer had ever been required to compel her children to school. It would have taken force to keep them away. But what of their future? Who can say? But of one thing I am very sure, and it is this: that, given fair opportunity, the whole family will adorn any station of life that they may be called to fill.

But will they have that opportunity? Well, the friend that was with me says they will, and he has commissioned me to act for him, promising me that if I am taken first and he is left, the cultured family of the slums shall not go uncared for. And amidst the sordid life of our mean streets, there are numbers of brilliant children whose God-given talents not only run to waste, but are actually turned into evil for lack of opportunity.

Here and there one and another rise superior to their environment, and with splendid perseverance fight their way to higher and better life. And some of them rise to eminence, for genius is not rare even in Slumdom.

One of our greatest artists, lately dead, whose work all civilisation delights to honour, played in a slum gutter, and climbed a lamp-post that he might get a furtive look into a school of art.

All honour and good wishes to the rising young, but all glory to the half-starved widows who shape their characters and form their tastes. To the old shoemaker good wishes; may the small pension that a friend of mine has settled on him add to his comfort and his health, may his beloved minor poets with Dickens and Shakespeare long be dear to him, and may his poor little home long continue to be peopled with bright creations that defy the almost omnipotent power of the underworld.

If any who may read these words would like to do a kind action that will not be void of good results and sure reward, I would say lend a helping hand to some poor family where, in spite of their poverty and surroundings, the children are clean and intelligent, and have made progress at school. For they are just needing a hand, it may be to help with their education, or it may be to give them a suitable start in life. If the mother happens to be a widow, you cannot do wrong.

If one half of the money that is spent trying to help unhelpable people was spent in helping the kind of families I refer to in the manner I describe, the results would be surprising.

If there is any difficulty in finding such families, I would say apply to the head mistress or master of a big school in a poor neighbourhood, they can find them for you. If they cannot, why then I will from among my self-supporting widow friends.

But do not, I beseech you, apply to the clergyman of the parish, for he will naturally select some poor family to whom he has charitably acted the part of relieving officer. Remember it is brains and grit that you are in search of, and not poor people only.

If in every neighbourhood a few people would band themselves together for this purpose and spend money for this one charitable purpose, it would of itself, and in reasonable time, effect mighty results. Believe me, there is plenty of brain power and grit in the underworld that never gets a chance of developing in a useful direction. Boys and girls possessing such talents are doomed, unless a miracle happens, for they have to start in life anyhow and anywhere.

Nothing is of more importance than a correct start in life for any boy or girl; but a false start, a bad beginning for the children of the very poor who happen to possess brain power is fatal. Their talents get no chance, for they are never used, consequently they atrophy, or, worse still, are used in a wrong direction and possibly for evil. Good is changed into evil, bright and useful life is frustrated, and the State loses the useful power and influence that should result from brains and grit.

How can my widow friends, who are unceasingly at work, have either the time, opportunity or knowledge to find proper openings for their children? The few shillings that a boy or girl can earn at anything, or anyhow that is honest, are a great temptation. The commencement dominates the future! Prospective advantage must needs give place to present requirements.

So we all lose! The upperworld loses the children's gifts, character and service. The underworld retains their poor service for life.

"It is better," said Milton, "to kill a man than a book." Which may be true, but probably the truth depends upon the quality of the man and the book. But what about killing mind, soul, heart, aspirations and every quality that goes to make up a man? "Their angels do always behold the face of my Father"; yes, but we compel them to withdraw that gaze, and look contentedly into the face of evil.

I am now pleading for the gifted boys and girls of the underworld, not the weaklings, for of them I speak elsewhere. But I will say, that while the weaklings are the more hopeless, it is the talented that are the most dangerous. Let us see to it that their powers have some chance of developing in a right direction. When by some extraordinary concurrence of circumstances a Council School boy passes on to a university and takes a good degree, it is chronicled all over the world; the school, the teacher, the boy and his parents are all held up for show and admiration. I declare it makes me ill! Why? Because I know that in the underworld thousands of men are grubbing, burrowing and grovelling who, as boys, possessed phenomenal abilities, but whose parents were poor, so poor that their gifted children had no chance of developing the talent that was in them. Let us give them a chance! Sometimes here and there one and another bursts his bonds, and, rejoicing in his freedom, does brilliant things. But in spite of Samuel Smiles and his self-help they are but few, though, if the centuries are searched, the catalogue will be impressive enough.

Of course there must be self-help. But there must be opportunity also. There is a great deal of talk about the children of the poor being "over-educated," and the delinquencies of the youthful poor are attributed to this bogy. It is because they are under-educated, not over-educated, that the children of the very poor so often go wrong.

But the attempt to cast them all in the same mould is disastrous; there is an over-education going on in this direction. Not all the children of the poor can be great scholars, but some of them can! Let us give them a chance. Not all of them can be scientists and engineers, etc., but some of them have talents for such things! Give them a chance! A good many of them have unmistakably artistic gifts! Why not give them a chance too! And the mechanically inclined should have a chance! Why can we not differentiate according to their tastes and gifts?

For even then we shall have enough left to be our hewers of wood and carriers of water; an abundance will remain to do all the work that requires neither brains nor gifts.

But let us stop at once and for ever trying to cram thick heads and poor brains with stuff that cannot possibly be appreciated or understood. Let us teach their mechanical fingers to do something useful, and give them, even the degenerates, some chance!

And we must stop our blind alley occupation for growing lads, for at the end of the alley stands an open door to the netherworld, and through it youthful life passes with little prospect of return.

X

Play in the Underworld

It may seem a strange thing, but children do play in the underworld. They have their own games and their times and seasons too!

Yet no one can watch them as they play without experiencing feelings more or less pathetic. There is something incongruous about it that may cause a smile, but there is also something that will probably cause a tear.

For their playgrounds are the gutters or the pavements. Happy are the children when they can procure a spacious pavement, for in the underworld wide pavements are scarce; still narrow pavements and gutters are always to hand.

It is summer time, the holidays have come! No longer the hum, babble and shouts of children are heard in and around those huge buildings, the County Council schools.

The sun pours its rays into the unclean streets, the thermometer registers eighty in the shade. Down from the top storey and other storeys of the blocks the children come, happy in the consciousness that for one month at least they will be free from school, without dodging the school attendance officer.

"Hop-scotch" season has commenced, and as if by magic the pavements of the narrow streets are covered with chalked lines, geometrical figures and numerals, and the mysterious word "tod" confronts you, stares at you, and puzzles you.

Who can understand the intricacies of "hop-scotch" or the fascination of "tod"? None but the girls of the underworld. Simple pleasures please them—a level pavement, a piece of chalk, a "pitcher," the sun overhead, dirt around, a few companions and non-troublesome babies, are their chief requirements; for few of these girls come out to play without the eternal baby.

Notice first, if you will, how deftly these foster-mothers handle the babies; their very method tells of long-continued practice. What slaves these girls are! But they have brought the baby's feeding-bottle, and also that other fearsome indispensable of underworld infant life, "the comforter."

They are going to make a day of it, a mad and merry day, for they have with them some pieces of bread and margarine to sustain them in the toil of nursing and the exhaustion of "hop-scotch."

The "pitcher" is produced, and we notice how punctiliously each girl takes her proper turn and starts from the correct place; we notice also the dilapidated condition of their boots, that act as golf clubs and propel the "pitcher." We wonder how with such boots, curled and twisted to every conceivable shape, they can strike the "pitcher" at all. There is some skill in "hop-scotch" played as these girls play it, and with their "boots" too!

A one-legged game is "hop-scotch," for the left foot must be held clear of the pavement, and the "pitcher" must be propelled with the right foot as the girl "hops."

If she hops too high and misses it, she is "out"; if she strikes too hard, and it travels beyond one of the boundaries, she is "out" too; if she does not propel it far enough, again "out."

Why, of course there is skill and fascination in it, for it combines the virtues of golf and baseball, and "tod" is quite as good as a football goal. And there is good fellowship and self-denial going on, too; not quite every girl, thank Heaven, is hampered or blessed with a baby, and we notice how cheerfully they take their turn in nursing while the foster-mother arrives at "tod."

The substitute, too, understands the use of the "comforter," for should it roll in the dirty gutter she promptly returns it to its proper place, the baby's mouth. Untidy, slatternly girls, not over-clean, not over-dressed, and certainly not over-fed, we leave them to their play and their babies.

Here are a lot of half-naked boys, some standing, some sitting on the hot pavement; they are playing "cherry hog"; why "hog" I don't know! Their requisites are a pocketful of cherry stones and a small screw, not an expensive outfit, for they save the "hogs" when they are permitted to eat cherries, as sometimes, by the indulgence of a kindly fruiterer, they are, for he kindly throws all his rotten or unsaleable fruit into the gutter.

If these are not to hand, there are plenty of "hogs" to be picked up. As to the little screw, well, it is easy to get one or steal one.

The advantage of a screw is that it possesses a flat end, on which it will stand erect. In this position it is delicately placed so that when struck by a cherry "hog" it falls. Each boy in turn throws a certain number of "hogs" at the screw, the successful thrower gathers in the spoil and goes home with his pocket bursting with cherry "hogs."

It's an exciting game, but it is gambling nevertheless; why do not the police interfere?

Here are some boys playing "buttons"—gambling again! This game is good practice, too, and a capital introduction to that famous game of youthful capitalists, "pitch and toss," for it is played in precisely the same way, only that buttons take the place of half-pennies.

The road, gutter or pavement will do for "buttons"; a small mark or "jack" is agreed upon, a line is drawn at a certain distance; alternately the lads pitch their buttons towards the "jack," three buttons each. When all have "pitched," the boy whose button is nearest the "jack" has first toss, that is, he collects all the pitched buttons in his hand and tosses them; as the buttons lie again on the ground the lads eagerly scan them, for the buttons that lie with their convex side upwards are the spoil of the first "tosser." The remaining buttons are collected by the second, who tosses, and then collects his spoil, and so on till the buttons are all lost and won. The boy whose buttons are farthest from "jack" of course gets the last and least opportunity. When playing for halfpence, "heads or tails" is the deciding factor.

Why, you say, of course it is a game of skill, just as much as bowls or quoits; but there are also elements of luck about "pitch and toss" which gives it an increased attraction.

Sunday in the underworld is the great day for "pitch and toss," for many boys have halfpence on that day. They have been at work during the week, and, having commenced work, their Sunday-school days are at an end. And having a few halfpence they can indulge their long-continued and fervent hope of discarding "buttons" and playing the man by using halfpence.

But how they enjoy it! how intent they are upon it. Sunday morning will turn to midday, and midday to evening before they are tired of it! Meal times, or the substitute for meal times, pass, and they remain at it! always supposing their halfpence last, and the police do not interfere, the latter being the most likely.

It takes an interminably long time to dispossess a lad of six halfpence at this game; fortune is not so fickle as may be supposed. The unskilled "pitcher" may have luck in "tossing," while the successful "pitcher" may be an unlucky "tosser." If at the end of a long day they come off pretty equal, they have had an ideal day.

But they have had their ups and downs, their alternations of joy and despair. Sometimes a boy may win a penny; if so, it is evident that another boy has lost one, and this is sad, though I expect they lose more coppers to the police than they do to their companions, for the police harry them and hunt them. Special constables are put on to detect them, and they know the favourite resorts of the incipient gamblers. They hunt in couples, too, and they enter the little unclean street at each end.

Now for the supreme excitement; they are observed by the watchful eye of a non-player, who is copperless. There is a rush for the halfpence, some of which the non-player secures. There's a scamper, but there is no escape; the police bag them, and innocent boys who join in the scamper are bagged too. The police search the ground for halfpence, find a few which they carefully pack in paper, that they may retain some signs of dirt upon them, for this will be invaluable legal evidence on the morrow. There is a procession of police, prisoners and gleeful lads who are not in custody to the nearest police-station.

On Monday they stand in the dock, when the police with the half-pence and the dirt still upon them give evidence against them.

One worthy magistrate will ask them why they were not at home or school. Another will sternly admonish them upon the evils of street gambling. A third will tell them that it would have paid them better in health and pocket to have taken a country walk. But all agree on one point, "that this street gambling must be put down," and they "put it down," or attempt to do so, by fining the young ragamuffins five shillings each.

The excitement of the cells then awaits them, to be followed by a free ride in "Black Maria," unless "muvver" can pawn something and raise the money, But many mothers cannot do this, others do not trouble; as to "farver," well, he does not come in at all, unless it is to give a "licking" to the boy when he comes out of prison for losing his job and his wages.

Truly, the play of the underworld children is exciting enough: there is danger attaching to it; perhaps that gives a piquancy to it.

The fascination of "pitch and toss" is felt not only all over England, where it holds undisputed sway, for it has no real rival, but in America too! Whilst in America last summer I explored the mean streets of New York, and not far from the Bowery I found lots of lads at the game. It was Sunday morning, too, and having some "nickels," I played several games with them. I was but a poor pitcher, the coins were too light for me—perhaps I could do better with solid English pennies—but what I lost in pitching I gained in tossing, so I was not ruined, neither did the Bowery lads sustain any loss.

But I found the procedure exactly the same as in England, and I felt the fascination of it; and some day when I can afford it, I will have a lot of metal counters made, and I will organise lads into a club;

I will give them "caps," and they shall play where the police won't interfere.

I will give them trophies to contend for, and Bethnal Green shall contend with Holloway; a halfpenny "gate" would bring its thousands, and private gain would give place to club and district "esprit de corps," for the lads want the game, not the money; the excitement, not the halfpence. There is nothing intrinsically wrong about "pitch and toss," only the fact that ragamuffins play it.

There is a great deal of nonsense talked about the game by superior people who pose as authorities upon the delinquencies of ragamuffin youth, and who declaim upon the demoralisation attending this popular game of poor lads.

I heard at a meeting of a rich Christian Church, held in a noble hall in the heart of London's City, one gentleman declare that a smart ragamuffin youth of his acquaintance possessed a penny with a "head" on each side for the purpose of enabling him to cheat at this game.

He did not know what he was talking about, for such pennies would be as useless for this game as the stones in the streets, for "heads and tails" are the essence of the game. The boys of the underworld must play, and ought to play; if those above them do not approve of their games, well, it is "up to them," as the Americans have it, to find them better games than pitch and toss, and better playing grounds than unclean streets.

Of public parks we have enough; they are very well for sedate and elderly people. They are useful to foster-mothers, slave girls hugging babies about, and a boon for nurses with perambulators. But what of Tom, Dick and Harry, who have just commenced work; what of them? "Boy Scouting," even with royal patronage, is not for them, for they have no money to buy uniforms, nor time to scour Epping Forest and Hampstead Heath for a non-existent enemy.

Church Lads' Brigade with bishops for patrons, did I hear some one say? Well, blowing a bugle, no matter how discordantly, is certainly an attraction for a boy; and wearing a military cap set jauntily on one side of the head is attractive, too, while the dragging of a make-believe cannon through the streets may perhaps please others. But Tom, Dick and Harry from below care for none of these things, for they are "make-believes," and Tom, Dick and Harry want something real, even if it is vulgar, something with a strong competitive element in it, even if it is a little bit rough or wicked.

Besides Tom, Dick and Harry are not over-clean in person, nor nice in speech, so they are not wanted. Boy Scouts and Boys' Brigades are preached at, but Tom, Dick and Harry do not want to be preached at by a parson, or coddled by a curate.

They want something real, even though it be punching each other's head, for that at any rate is real. Give us play, play, real play! is the cry that is everlastingly rising from the underworld youth. But the overworld gives them parks and gardens, which are closed at a respectable hour. But the lads do not go to bed at respectable hours, for their mothers are still at work and their fathers have not arrived home. So they play in the streets; then we call them "hooligans," and of course they must be "put down."

There is a good deal of "putting down" for the underworld, but it is all of the wrong sort. For there is no putting down of public playgrounds for lads of fifteen and upwards open in the evening, lighted by electricity, and under proper control. Not one in the whole underworld. So they play in the streets, or rather indulge in what is called "horse-play."

But there are youths' clubs! Yes, a few mostly in pokey places, yet they are useful. But Tom, Dick and Harry want space, room and air, for they get precious little of these valuable commodities at their work, and still less in their homes. Watch them if you will, as I have watched them scores of times in the streets, how foolish, yet how pitiable their conduct is; you will see that they walk for about two hundred yards and then walk back again, and then repeat the same walk, till the hours have passed; they seem to be as circumscribed as caged animals. They walk within bounds up and down the "monkey's parade."

How inane and silly their conversation is! Sometimes a whim comes upon them, and one runs for a few yards; the whim takes possession of others, and they do exactly the same. One seizes another round the body and wrestles with him. Immediately the others begin to wrestle too; their actions are stereotyped, silly and objectionable, even when they do not quarrel.

They bump against the people, women included, especially young women. They push respectable people into the gutters, and respectable people complain to the police. An extra force is told off to keep order, and to put Tom, Dick and Harry down.

Sunday night is the worst night of all! for now these youths are out in their thousands; certain streets are given up to them, and become impassable for others. Respectable folk are shocked, and church-going folk are scandalised! Surely the streets are the property of respectable people! and yet they cannot pass through them without annoyance.

At length the street is cleared and patrolled, for respectability must be protected, not that there has been either violence or robbery. Oh dear, no! There has only been foolish horse-play by the Toms, Dicks and Harrys who, having nowhere else to go, and nothing else to do, having, moreover, been joined by their female counterparts, have been enjoying themselves in their own way, for they have been "at play."

It is astonishing how fond of water the unwashed children of the underworld are! It has an attraction for them, often a fatal attraction, even though it be thick with dirt and very malodorous. During the summer time the boys' bathing lakes in Victoria Park are crowded and alive with youngsters, who splash and flounder and choke, splutter and laugh in them. They present a sight worth seeing, and teach a lesson worth remembering.

The canals of Hoxton, Haggerston and Islington, too, dirty and dangerous as they are, prove seductive to the boys who live close to them. Now the police have an anxious time. Again they must look after Tom, Dick and Harry, for demure respectability must not be outraged by a sight of their naked bodies.

So the police keep a sharp outlook for them. Some one kindly informs them that a dozen boys are bathing in the canal near a certain bridge, and quickly enough they find them in the very act. There the little savages are! Some can swim, and some cannot; those that cannot are standing in the slime near the side, stirring up its nastiness. They see the policeman advancing, and those that can swim get ashore and run for their little bits of clothing, tied up in a bundle ready for emergencies. Into the water again they go for the other side! But, alas! another policeman is waiting on the other side at the place where they expected to land, so they must needs swim till another landing place offers security. But even here they find that escape is hopeless, for yet another policeman awaits them.

Those who cannot swim seize their bundles, and, without waiting to dress, run naked and unashamed along the canal, side, to the merriment of the bargees, and the joy of the women and girls who happen to have no son or brother amongst them, for the underworld is not so easily shocked as the law and its administrators imagine.

Ultimately they, too, find a policeman waiting for them, and a "good bag" results. But the magistrate is very lenient; with a twinkle in his eye he reproves them, and fines them one shilling each, which with great difficulty their "muvvers" pay.

But it has been a good day for the police, for four of them have helped to convey six shillings from the wretchedly poor to the coffers of the police-court receiver. But when the school holidays come round, that is the time for the dirty canal to tell its tale, and to give up its dead, too!

Read this from the Daily Press, July 16th, 1911—

"A remarkable record in life-saving was disclosed at a Bethnal Green inquest to-day on a child of six, named Browning, who was drowned in the Regent's Canal on Bank Holiday.

"Henry H. Terry, an out-of-work carman, said he was called from his home near by, and raced down to the canal. There was a youth on

146

the bank holding a stick over the water, apparently waiting for the child to come up to the surface.

"The coroner: 'How old was the youth?' 'Well, he stood five feet six inches, and might have gone in without getting out of his depth. I heard a woman cry, "Why don't you go in!" I dived in five or six times, but did not bring up the body.' The witness added that he and his brother had saved many lives at this spot, the latter having effected as many as twenty-five rescues in a year. Alfred Terry, a silk weaver, described the point at which the child was drowned as a veritable death-trap, and mentioned that he had been instrumental during the past twelve years in saving considerably over one hundred lives at that spot.

"'One hot July afternoon in 1900,' he added,'my mother and I had five of them in the kitchen at one time with a roaring fire to bring them round. That was during the school holidays; they dropped in like flies.'

"Accidental death was the verdict."

But when the little ones play in the gutter, danger lurks very near, as witness the extract of the same date—

"At an inquest at the Poplar coroner's court to-day, on a three-years'-old girl named Bertiola, it was stated that while playing with other children she was struck on the head with a tin engine. Three weeks later she was playing with the same children, and one of them hit her on the head with the wooden horse.

"The coroner: 'Two similar blows in a few days, that is very strange.'

"Dr. Packer said that death was due to cerebral meningitis, the result of a blow on the head.

"The coroner: 'I suppose you can't tell which blow caused the trouble' 'No, sir, I am afraid not.'

"The jury returned a verdict of accidental death."

But sometimes the boys and girls of the underworld collaborate in their play, for just now (July) "Remember the grotto! please to remember the grotto!" is a popular cry. Who has not seen the London grottos he who knows them not, knows nothing of the London poor.

I was watching some girls play "hop-scotch" when a boy and girl with oyster shells in their hands came up to me preferring the usual request, "Please to remember the grotto!" Holding out their shells as they spoke.

"Where is your grotto?" I said. "There, sir, over there; come and see it." Aye! there is was, sure enough, and a pretty little thing it was in its way, built up to the wall in a quiet corner, glistening with its oyster shells, its bits of coloured china and surmounted with a little flag.

"But where are the candles?" "Oh, sir, we haven't got any yet; we shall get candles when we get some money, and light them to-night; we have only just finished it." "Where did you get your shells?" "From the fish-shops." "Where did you get the pretty bits of china from?" "We saved them from last year." "Does grotto time come the same time every year,then" "Oh yes, sir." "How is that?" " 'Cos it's the time for it." "Why do you build grottos" "To get money." "Yes, but why do people give you money; what do grottos commemorate, don't you know?" "No, sir."

I looked at a poor half-paralysed boy with sharp face and said, "Well, my boy, you ought to know; do you go to Sunday School?" "Yes, sir, both of us; St. James the Less." "Well, I shall not tell you the whole story to-day, but here is sixpence for you to buy candles with; and next Sunday ask your teacher to tell you why boys and girls build grottos; I shall be here this day week, and if you can tell me I will give you a shilling."

There were at least six grottos in that street when I got there on the appointed day. A large crowd of children with oyster shells were waiting; evidently the given sixpence and the promised shilling had created some excitement in that corner of Bethnal Green,

They were soon all round me, and a general chorus arose with hands outstretched, "Please to remember the grotto! please to remember the grotto! "I called them to silence, and said, "Can any one tell me why you build grottos?" There was a general chorus, "To get money, sir." That was all they knew, and it seemed to them a sufficient reason.

148

Turning to the little cripple, I said, "Did you ask your teacher?" "Yes, sir, but she said it was only children's play; but I bought some candles, and they are lighted now."

I said, "Now, children, listen to me, for I am going to tell you about the beginning of grottos.

"A good many hundred years ago, when Jesus was on earth, He had two disciples named James; in after years one was called 'James the Greater' and the other 'James the Less.' After the death of Jesus, James the Greater was put to death, and the disciples were scattered, and wandered into many far countries. James the Less wandered into Spain, telling the people about Jesus. He lived a good and holy life, helping the poor and the afflicted.

"When he died, the people who loved him and reverenced him made a great funeral, and built him a costly tomb, but instead of putting up a monument to him, they built a large and beautiful grotto over the place where his body lay. They lined it with beautiful and costly shells and other rich things, and lit it with many candles.

"Thousands of people came to see the grotto, and gave money to buy candles that it might always be lighted.

"Every year, on the anniversary of St. James's death, the people came by thousands to the grotto. One year it was said that a crippled man had been made quite well while praying at the grotto. This event was told everywhere, and from that day forth on St. James's Day people came from many countries, many of them walking hundreds of miles to the grotto.

"Some of these people were ill and diseased, and others were sick and blind, and some were cripples.

"It is said that a good many of them were cured of their afflictions.

"Now all these poor people that walked slowly and painfully to St. James's tomb carried big oyster shells, in which they made holes for cords to pass through, and they placed the cords round their necks.

"When they came near to people they would hold out their shells and say, 'Please to remember the grotto!' And people gave them money to help them on their way and to buy candles for the grotto, hoping that the poor people would get there safely and come back cured.

So it came to pass that whenever people saw a man with an oyster shell, they knew he was going or returning from St. James's tomb in Spain, and they helped him. The custom of building grottos on St. James's Day spread to many countries besides Spain. In Russia they build very fine grottos. At length the custom came to England, and you boys and girls do what other boys and girls have done for many years in other countries, and in reality you celebrate the death of a great and good man."

The children were very silent for a while; the cripple boy looked at me with tears in his eyes, and I knew what his tears expressed. I gave him a shilling, but he did not speak; to all the other children who had built grottos I gave threepence each, and there was joy in that corner of Bethnal Green.

There is always something pathetic about play in the underworld. We feel that there is something wanting in it, perhaps that something would come into it, if there were more opportunities of real and competitive play. Keeping shops, or teaching schools may do for girls to play at, but a lad, if he is any good, wants something more robust.

I often find cripple boys playing "tip-cat," another game upon which the law has its eye, or hurrying along on crutches after something that serves as a football, and getting there in time, too, for a puny kick. But that kick, little as it is, thrills the poor chap, and he feels that he has been playing. I am sure that football is going to play a great part in the physical salvation of Tom, Dick and Harry, but they must have other places than the streets in which to learn and practise the game.

We have heard a great deal about the playing-fields of public schools; we are told that we owe our national safety to them; perhaps it is correct, but I really do not know. But this I do know, that the non-provision of playing-fields, or grounds for the male youthful poor, is a national danger and a menace to activity, endurance, health and pluck.

Nothing saves them now but the freehold of the streets. Rob them of this without giving them something better, and we shall speedily have a race of flat-footed, flat-chested, round-shouldered poor, with no brains for mental work, and no strength for physical work. A race exactly qualified for the conditions to which we so freely submit it in prison. And above those conditions that race will have no aspirations. So give them play, glorious play, manly strife; let their hearts beat, and their chests expand that they may breathe from their bottom lungs, that their limbs may be supple and strong, for it will pay the nation to give Tom, Dick and Harry healthy play.

And they long for it, do Tom, Dick and Harry! Did you ever see hundreds of them on a Sunday morning coming up from their lairs in Hoxton, Shoreditch, Spitalfields and Bethnal Green, to find a field or open space in the suburbs where they might kick a football? I have seen it scores of times. A miserable but hopeful sight it is; hopeful because it bears testimony to the ingrained desire that English lads have for active healthy play. Miserable because of their appearance, and because of the fact that no matter what piece of open ground or fields they may select, they are trespassers, and may be ejected, or remain on sufferance only.

Happy are they if they can find a piece of land marked for sale, where the jerry-builder has not yet commenced a suburban slum. Like a swarm of locusts they are down on it, and quickly every blade of grass disappears, "kicked off" as if by magic.

Old walking-sticks, pieces of lath or old coats and waistcoats serve as goal-posts. Touch-lines they have none, one playing-ground runs across the other, and a dozen teams are soon hard at it. They have no caps to distinguish them, no jerseys or knickers of bright hues. There are no "flannelled fools" among them, but quickly there are plenty of "muddied oafs." Trousers much too long are rolled up, coats and vests are dispensed with, braces are loosed and serve as belts. There is running to and fro, mud, and poor old footballs are kicked hither and thither. They knock, kick and shoulder each other, their bare arms and faces are coated with mud, they fall over the ball and over each other. If they cannot kick their own ball, they kick one that belongs to another team. There is much shouting, much laughter and some bad language! and so they go at it till presently there is a great cheer, for Hoxton has got a second goal, and Haggerston is defeated. And they keep at it for two long hours, if they are not interfered with, then back to their lairs and food.

All this time good people have been in the churches close by, and the shouting of the Hoxtonians has disturbed them, and the gentle whisper of the Haggerstonians has annoyed them. Some of them are scandalised, and say the police ought to stop such nuisances; perhaps they are right, for there is much to be said against it. But there is something to be said on the other side, too; for the natural instinct of English boys must have an outlet or perish. If it perish they perish too, and then old England would miss them.

So let them play, but give them playgrounds! For playgrounds will pay better than nice, respectable parks. The outlay will be returned in due time in a big interest promptly paid from the increased vitality, energy, industry and honesty of our Toms, Dicks and Harrys. So let them play!

With much pleasure I quote from the Daily Press, November 24th, the following—

"LEARNING TO PLAY
"ORGANISED GAMES IN HYDE PARK IN SCHOOL HOURS

"It is good news that arrangements are being made by the Office of Works for the use of a part of Hyde Park for organised games under the direction of the London County Council. Hitherto the only royal parks in which space has been allotted for this purpose are Regent's Park and Greenwich Park. But the King, as is well known, takes a keen interest in all that concerns the welfare of the children, and has gladly sanctioned the innovation.

"During the year an increasing number of the elementary schools in London have taken advantage of the article in the code of regulations which provides that, under certain conditions, organised games may, if conducted under competent supervision and instruction, be played during school hours. Up to the present the London County Council has authorised the introduction of organised games by 580 departments, 295 boys', 225 girls', and 60 mixed.

"The games chiefly played by boys are football, cricket and rounders, according to the season. Girls enjoy a greater variety, and in addition to cricket and rounders, are initiated into the mysteries of hockey, basket ball, target ball, and other ball games.

"The advantages of the children being taught to get the best exercise out of the games, and to become skilful in them, are obvious.

"Arrangements have been made with the various local athletic associations and consultative committees whereby in each metropolitan borough there are hon. district representatives (masters and mistresses) in connection with organised games. Pitches are reserved in over thirty of the L.C.C. parks and open spaces for the use of schools. The apparatus required is generally stored at the playing-fields for the common use of all schools attending, but small articles such as balls, bats, sticks are supplied to each school.

"The Council has decided that, so far as practicable, the apparatus for organised games shall be made at the Council's educational institutes, and, as a result of this decision, much of it is fashioned at the handicraft centres."

This is all for good. But I am concerned for adolescent youth that has left school—the lads whose home conditions absolutely prevent the evening hours being spent indoors. Is there to be no provision for them?

XI

On the Verge
of the Underworld

Charles Dickens has somewhere said, "The ties that bind the rich to their homes may be made on earth, but the ties that bind the poor to their homes are made of truer metal and bear the stamp of Heaven." And he adds that the wealthy may love their home because of the gold, silver and costly things therein, or because of the family history. But that when the poor love their homes, it is because their household gods are gods of flesh and blood. Dickens's testimony is surely true, for struggle, cares, sufferings and anxieties make their poor homes, even though they be consecrated with pure affection, "serious and solemn places."

To me it has always been evident that the heaviest part of the burden inseparable from a poor man's home falls upon the wife.

Blessed is that home where the wife is equal to her duties, and doubly blessed is the home where the husband, being a true helpmate, is anxious to carry as much of the burden as possible. For then the home, even though it be small and its floors brick, becomes in all truth "a sweetly solemn place." It becomes a good training ground for men and women that are to be. But I am afraid the working men do not sufficiently realise what heavy, onerous and persistent duties fall upon the wife. With nerves of brass they do not appreciate the fact that wives may be, and are, very differently constituted to themselves. Many wives are lonely; but the husbands do not always understand the gloomy imaginations that pervade the lonely hours. The physical laws that govern women's personal health make periods of depression and excitement not only possible, but certain.

Let us consider for a moment the life of a poor man's wife in London, where her difficulties are increased by high rent and a long absence of the husband. She has the four everlasting walls to look at, eternal anxieties as to the future, the repeated weekly difficulties of making ends meet, and too often the same lack of consideration from the husband.

The week's washing for the family she must do, the mending and darning for the household is her task, the children must be washed and clothed and properly cared for by her. Of her many duties there is no end.

Sickness in the family converts her into a nurse. She herself must bear the pangs and sufferings of motherhood, and for that time must make preparation. For death in the family she must also provide, so the eternities are her concern. Things present and things to come leave her little time to contemplate the past.

Ask me the person of many duties, and I point to the wife of a poor man.

Thank God, the law of compensation rules the universe, and she is not exempt from its ruling. She has her compensations doubtless, but I am seriously afraid not to the extent to which she is entitled, though, perhaps, they are greater than we imagine.

Her duties are not always pleasant, for when her husband falls out of work the rent must be paid, or she must mollify a disappointed landlord. In many of our London "model" dwellings, if she is likely to have a fourth child, three being the limit, she must seek a new home. And it ought to be known that on this account there is a great exodus every year from some of our London "dwellings."

It seems scarcely credible, but it is nevertheless a fact, that in some dwellings she may not keep a cat, a dog, or even a bird, neither may she have flowers in pots on her window-sills. She is hedged round with prohibitions, but she is expected to be superior and to abide in staid respectability on an income of less than thirty shillings per week. And she does it, though how she does it is a marvel.

Come with me to visit Mrs. Jones, who lives at 28, White Elephant Buildings. Mr. Jones is a painter at work for eight months in the year, if he has good luck, but out of work always at that time of the year when housekeeping expenses are highest. For every working man's wife will tell you that coal is always dearer at the time of the year when it is most required. In White Elephant Buildings there is no prohibition as to the number of children, or the Jones family would not be there, for they number eight all told. It is dinner time, and the children are all in from school, and, being winter time, Jones is at home too! He has been his wearying round in search of work earlier in the day, and has just returned to share the midday meal which the mother serves. In all conscience the meal is limited enough, but we notice that Jones gets an undue proportion, and we wonder whether the supply will go round.

We see that the children are next served in their order, the elder obtaining just a little more food than the younger, and, last of all—Mrs. Jones.

It is true that self-denial brings its own reward, for in her case there is little to reward her in the shape of food.

To me it is still astonishing, although I have known it for years, that thousands of poor men's wives go through years of hard work, and frequent times of motherhood on an amount of food that must be altogether inadequate.

Brave women! Aye, brave indeed! for they not only deny themselves food, but clothing, and all those little personal adornments that are so dear to the heart of women. There is no heroism to equal it. It only ends when the children have all passed out of hand, and then it is too late, for in her case appetite has not been developed with eating, so that when the day comes that food is more plentiful, the desire for it is lacking.

It is small wonder, then, that Mrs. Jones has a careworn look, and does not look robust. She has been married twelve years, so that every second year she has borne a child. The dark rings beneath her eyes tell of protracted hours of work, and the sewing-machine underneath the window tells us that she supplements the earnings of her husband by making old clothes into new, and selling them to her neighbours, either for their children's wear or their own. This accounts for the fact that her own children are so comfortably clothed. The dinner that we have seen disappear cost ninepence, for late last evening, just before the cheap butchers close by shut up for the night, Mrs. Jones bought one pound and a half of pieces, and, with the aid of two onions and some potatoes, converted them into a nourishing stew.

Many times near midnight I have stood outside the cheap butchers' and watched careful women make their purchases. It is a pitiful sight, and when one by one the women have made their bargains, we notice that the shopboard is depleted of its heap of scrags and odds and ends.

So day by day Mrs. Jones feeds her family, limiting her expenditure to her purse. And, truth to tell, Jones and the little Joneses look well on it. But two things in addition to the rent test her managing powers. Boots for the children! and coal for the winter! The latter difficulty she gets over by paying one shilling per week into a coal club all the year through. When Jones is in work she buys extra coal, but when the winter comes she draws upon her reserves at the coal merchant's.

But the boots are more difficult. To his credit let it be said that Jones mends the family's boots. That is, he can "sole and heel," though he cannot put on a patch or mend the uppers. But with everlasting thought for the future, Mrs. Jones makes certain of boots for the family. Again a "club" is requisitioned, and by dint of rigid management two shillings weekly pass into a shoemaker's hands, and in their turn the family gets boots; the husband first, the children one by one, herself last—or never!

Week by week she lives with no respite from anxiety, with no surcease from toil. By and by the eldest boy is ready for work, and Mrs. Jones looks forward to the few shillings he will bring home weekly, and builds great things upon it. Alas! it is not all profit; the boy must have a new suit, he requires more food, and he must have a little spending money, "like other boys"; and though he is a good lad, she finds ultimately that there is not much left of Tom's six shillings.

Never mind! on she goes, for will he not get a rise soon and again expectation encourages her.

So the poor woman, hampered as she is with present cares, looks forward to the time when life will be a bit easier, when the united earnings of the children will make a substantial family income. Oh, brave woman! it is well for her to live in hope, and every one who knows her hopes too that disappointment will not await her, and that her many children will "turn out well."

Mrs. Jones is typical of thousands of working men's wives, and such women demand our admiration and respect. What matter though some of them are a bit frowsy and not over-clean? they have precious little time to attend to their personal adornment. I ask, who can fulfil all their duties and remain "spick-and-span"?

"Nagging," did I hear some one say? My friend, put yourself in her place, and imagine whether you would remain all sweetness and courtesy. Again I say, that I cannot for the life of me understand how she can bear it all, suffering as she does, and yet remain so patient and so hopeful.

Add to the duties I have enumerated the time when sickness and death enter the home. Mrs. Grundy has declared that even poor people must put on "mourning," and must bury their dead with excessive expenditure, and Mrs. Grundy must be obeyed.

But what struggles poor wives make to do it! but a "nice" funeral is a fascinating sight to the poor. So thousands of poor men's wives deny themselves many comforts, and often necessaries, that they may for certain have a few pounds, should any of their children die. Religiously they pay a penny or twopence a week for each of their children to some industrial insurance company for this purpose.

A few pounds all at once loom so large that they forget all the toil, stress and self-denial they have undergone to keep those pence regularly paid. Decent "mourning" and "nice funerals" are greatly admired, for if a working man's wife accepts parish aid at such time, why then she has fallen low indeed.

And for the time when a new life comes into light, the poor man's wife must make provision. At this time anxiety is piled upon anxiety. There must be no parish doctor, no parish nurse; out of her insufficient income she makes weekly payments to a local dispensary that during sickness the whole household may be kept free of doctor's bills. An increased payment for herself secures her, when her time comes, from similar worry. But the nurse must be paid, so during the time of her "trouble" the poor woman screws, schemes and saves a little money; money that ought in all truth to have been spent upon herself, that a weekly nurse may attend her. But every child is dearer than the last, and the wonderful love she has for every atom of humanity born to her repays all her sufferings and self-denial.

So I ask for the poor man's wife not only admiration and consideration, but, if you will, some degree of pity also. I would we could make her burdens easier, her sorrows less, and her pleasures more numerous. Most devoutly I hope that the time may soon arrive when "rent day" will be less dreaded, and when the collector will be satisfied with a less proportion of the family's earnings. For this is a great strain upon the poor man's wife, a strain that is never absent! for through times of poverty and sickness, child birth and child death, persistently and inexorably that day comes round. Undergoing constant sufferings and ceaseless anxieties, it stands to the poor man's wife's credit that their children fight our battles, people our colonies, uphold the credit of our nation, and perpetuate the greatness of the greatest empire the world has ever known.

But Mrs. Jones' eldest girl has a hard time too! for she acts as nurse and foster-mother to the younger children. It was well for her that Tom was born before her or she would have nursed him. Perhaps it was well for Tom also that he got the most nourishment. As it is the girl has her hands full, and her time is more than fully occupied. She goes to school regularly both Sunday and week-day. She passes all her standards, although she is not brilliant. She washes the younger children, she nurses the inevitable baby, she clears the "dinner things" away at midday, and the breakfast and tea-cups in their turn. She sits down to the machine sometimes and sews the clothing her mother has cut out and "basted." She is still a child, but a woman before her time, and Mrs. Jones and all the young Joneses will miss her when she goes "out."

When that time comes, Mrs. Jones will not be so badly put to it as she was when Tom went "out." For she has been paying regularly into a draper's club, and with the proceeds a quantity of clothing material will be bought. So Sally's clothing will be made at home, and Sally and her mother will sit up late at night to make it.

It is astonishing how "clubs" of all descriptions enter into the lives of the poor. There is, of course, the "goose club" for Christmas, for the poor make sure of one good meal during the year. Some of them are extravagant enough to join "holiday clubs," but this Mrs. Jones cannot afford, so her clubs are limited to her family's necessities, excepting the money club held at a neighbour's house into which she pays one shilling weekly. This club consists of twenty members, who "draw" for choice. Thus once in twenty weeks, sooner or later, Mrs. Jones is passing rich, for she is in possession of twenty shillings all at once.

There is some discussion between Sally and her mother as to the spending of it; Tom's first suit was bought by this means, and Jones himself is not forgotten; but for Mrs. Jones no thought is given.

The planning, scheming and contrivance it takes to run a working man's home, especially when the husband has irregular work, is almost past conception, and the amount of self-denial is extraordinary.

But it is the wife who finds the brains and exercises the self-denial. Her methods may be laughed at by wiser people, for there is some wastage. The friendly club-keeper must have a profit, and the possession of wealth represented by a whole sovereign costs something. But when Mrs. Jones gets an early "draw," she exchanges her "draw" for a later one, and makes some little profit.

Oh, the scheming and excitement of it all, for even Mrs. Jones cannot do without her little "deal." But what will Sally settle down to? Now comes the difficulty and deciding point in her life, and a critical time it is.

Mrs. Jones has not attended a mother's meeting, she has been too busy; church has not seen much of her except at the christenings; district visitors and clergymen have not shown much interest in her; Jones himself is almost indifferent, and quite complacent.

So Sally and her mother discuss the matter. The four shillings weekly to be obtained in a neighbouring factory are tempting, but the girls are noisy and rude; yet Sally will be at home in the evenings and have time to help her mother, and that is tempting too! A neighbouring blouse-maker takes girls to teach them the trade, and Sally can machine already, so she will soon pick up the business; that looks nice too, but she would earn nothing for the first three months, so that is ruled out. Domestic service is thought of, but Sally is small for her age, and only fourteen; she does not want to be a nurse girl; she has had enough nursing—she has been a drudge long enough.

So to the factory she goes, though Mrs. Jones has her misgivings, and gives her strong injunctions to come straight home, which of course Sally readily promises, though whether that promise will be strictly kept is uncertain. But her four shillings are useful in the family exchequer; they are the deciding factor in Sally's life!

So on through all the succeeding years of the developing family life comes the recurring anxiety of getting her children "out." These anxieties may be considered very small, but they are as real, as important, and as grave as the anxieties that well-to-do people experience in choosing callings or professions for sons and daughters to whom they cannot leave a competency.

And all this time the family are near, so very near to the underworld. The death of Jones, half-timer as he is, would plunge them into it; and the breakdown or death of Mrs. Jones would plunge them deeper still.

What an exciting and anxious life it really is! Small wonder that many descend to the underworld when accident overtakes them. But for character, grit, patience and self-denial commend me to such women. All honour to them! may their boys do well! may their girls in days to come have less anxieties and duties than fall to the lot of working men's wives of to-day.

XII

In Prisons OFT

If every chapter in this book is ignored, I hope that this one will be read thoughtfully. For I want to show that a great national wrong, a stupidly cruel wrong, exists.

Probably all injustice is stupid, but this wrong is so foolish, that any man who thinks for one moment upon it will wonder how it came into existence.

I have written and spoken about it so often that I am almost ashamed of returning to the subject. Yet all our penal authorities, from the Home Secretary downwards, know all there is to be known about it.

I am going, then, to reiterate a serious charge! It is this: no boy from eight years of age up to sixteen, unless sound in mind and body, can find entrance into any reformatory or industrial school! No matter how often he falls into the hands of the police, or what charges may be brought against him, not even if he is friendless and homeless. Again, no youthful prisoner under twenty-one years of age, no matter how bad his record, is allowed the benefit of Borstal training unless he, too, be sound in mind and body. This is not only an enormity, but it is also a great absurdity; for it ultimately fills our prisons with weaklings, and assures the nation a continuous prison population.

It seems very extraordinary that prison and prison alone should be considered the one and only place suitable for the afflicted children of the poor when they break any law, but so it is.

The moral hump is tolerated, even patronised in reformative institutions, but the physical hump, never!

Cunning, dishonesty and rascality generally may be tolerated, but feebleness of mind or infirmity of body never! All through our penal administration and prison discipline this principle prevails, and is strictly acted upon.

Let me put it briefly; prison, and prison only, is the one and only place for afflicted youth when it happens to break one or the other of our laws.

We have numerous institutions, half penal and half educative, that exist absolutely for the purpose of receiving homeless, wayward or criminally inclined youthful delinquents.

These institutions, I say, although kept going from public funds, refuse, absolutely refuse, to give training to any youthful delinquent who suffers from physical infirmity or mental weakness.

Think of it again! all youthful delinquents suffering from any infirmity of body or mind, are refused reformative treatment or training in all publicly supported institutions established for delinquent youth.

He may be a thief, but if he is a hunchback they will have none of him. He may be a danger to other children, if he has fits he will not be received. He may rob the tills of small shopkeepers, but if he is lame, half-blind, has heart disease, or if his brain is not sound and his body strong, if he has lost a hand, got a wooden leg, if he suffers from any disease or deprivation, prison, and prison only, is the place for him. So to prison the afflicted one goes if over fourteen; if under fourteen back to his home, to graduate in due time for prison.

This is no exaggeration, it is a true picture, and this procedure has gone on till our prisons have become filled with broken and hopeless humanity.

Could any one ever suggest a more disastrous course than this? Why, decency, pity, or just a grain of common sense ought to teach us, and would teach us if we thought for a moment, that it is not only wrong but supremely foolish.

For there is a very close connection between neglected infirmity, mental or physical, and crime, a connection that ought to be considered, and few questions demand more instant attention. Yet no question is more persistently avoided and shelved by responsible authorities, for no means of dealing with the defective in mind or body when they commit offences against the law, other than by short terms of useless imprisonment, have at present been attempted or suggested. It seems strange that in Christianised, scientised England such procedure should continue even for a day, but continue it does, and to-day it seems as little likely to be altered as it was twenty years ago. Let me then charge it upon our authorities that they are responsible for perpetuating this great and cruel wrong. They are not in ignorance, for the highest authorities know perfectly well that every year many hundreds of helpless and hopeless degenerates or defectives are committed to prison and tabulated as habitual criminals. Our authorities even keep a list on which is placed the names of these unfortunates who, after prolonged experience and careful medical examinations, are found to be "unfit for prison discipline."

This list is of portentous length, and to it four hundred more names are added every year. This is of itself an acknowledgment by the State that every year four hundred unfortunate human beings who cannot appreciate the nature and quality of the acts they have committed, are treated, punished and graded as criminals. Now the State knows perfectly well that these unfortunates need pity, not punishment; the doctor, not the warder; and some place where mild, sensible treatment and permanent restraint can take the place of continual rounds of short imprisonment alternated with equally senseless short spells of freedom.

No! not freedom, but a choice between starvation, prison or workhouse. Now this list grows, and will continue to grow just so long as the present disastrous methods are persisted in!

Why does this list grow? Because magistrates have no power to order the detention of afflicted youthful offenders in any place other than prison; they cannot commit to reformatory schools only on sufferance and with the approval of the school managers, who demand healthy boys.

So ultimately to prison the weaklings go, and an interminable round of small sentences begins. But even in prison they are again punished because of their afflictions, for only the sound in mind and body are given the benefit of healthy life and sensible training.

Consequently in prison they learn little that can be of service to them; they only graduate in idleness, and prison having comforts but no terrors, they quickly join the ranks of the habitués. When it is too late they are "listed" as not suitable for prison treatment. Year by year in a country of presumably sane people this deplorable condition of things continues, and I am bold enough to say that there will be no reduction in the number of our prison population till proper treatment, training, and, if need be, detention, is provided in places other than prison for our afflicted youthful population when they become offenders against the law.

But reformatory and industrial schools have not only power to refuse youthful delinquents who are unsound in mind or body; they have also the power to discharge as "unfit for training" any who have managed to pass the doctor's examination, whose defects become apparent when under detention.

From the last Official Report of Reformatory Schools in England and Wales I take the following figures—

During the years 1906-7-8 14 imbeciles (males) were discharged on licence from reformatory schools; and during the same three years no less than 93 (males) were discharged by the Home Secretary's permission as "unfit for physical training." The 14 imbeciles in the Official Report are classified as dead, and the 93 physically unfit are included among them "not in regular employment."

For the same period of years I find that 28 (girls) were discharged from English reformatory schools as being physically unfit.

The Official Report of Industrial Schools includes England, Wales and Scotland, and for the same three years I find that 13 (males) were discharged from industrial schools as being imbeciles, and 116 (males) as being "unfit for physical training."

Strange to say, in the Annual Report the physically unfit are included among those "in casual employment," and the imbeciles are included among the "dead."

From the same Official Report we have the statement that in one year, 1909, in England and Scotland 991 (males) and 20 (females) who had been discharged from reformatory schools were re-convicted and committed to prison.

How many of them were mentally or physically defective we have no means of knowing, for no information is given upon this point; but there is not the slightest doubt that a large number of them were weak-minded, though not sufficiently so to allow them being classified as imbeciles.

The terrible consequence of this procedure may also be gathered from the Report of the Prison Commissioners for England and Wales 1910, from which it appears that during the year 157 persons were certified insane among the prisoners in the local and convict prisons, Borstal institutions and of State reformatories, during the year ending March 31, 1910.

In addition to the above there were 290 (213 males and 77 females) cases of insanity in remanded and other unconvicted prisoners dealt with during the year, including 14 males and 2 females found "insane on arraignment," and 173 males and 65 females found insane on remand from police or petty sessional courts. There were 30 (20 males and 10 females) prisoners found "guilty" but "insane" at their trial.

But the most illuminating report comes from the medical officer at Parkhurst Convict Prison; these are his words—

Weak-minded convicts and others whose mental state is doubtful continue to be collected here. The special rules for their management are adhered to. The number classified as weak-minded at the end of the year was 117, but in addition there were 34 convicts attached to the parties of weak-minded for further mental observation.

"The conduct and tractability of these prisoners naturally vary with the individual; a careful consideration of the history of each of the 117 classified weak-minded convicts indicates that about 64 are fairly easily managed, the remainder difficult to deal with, and a few are dangerous characters.

CLASSIFICATION OF WEAK-MINDED CONVICTS:—

(a) Congenital deficiency:-
    1. With epilepsy. 9
    2. Without epilepsy. 46
(b) Imperfectly developed stage of insanity. 18
(c) Mental debility after attack of insanity 8
(d) Senility. 2
(e) Alcohol. 6
(f) Undefined 28
 117

"The following is a list of the crimes of the classified weak-minded for which they are undergoing their present sentences of penal servitude, and the number convicted for each type of crime—

False pretences 3
Receiving stolen property 3
Larceny. 18
Burglary. 7
Shop-breaking, house-breaking, etc. 19
Uttering counterfeit coins 1
Threatening letters 4
Threatening violence to superior officer 1
Robbery with violence 3
Manslaughter 6
Wounding with intent 8
Grievous bodily harm 2
Attempted murder 1
Wilful murder 7
Rape 5
Carnal knowledge of little girls 8
Arson 15

"During the year 35 convicts were certified insane; of these 27 were removed to the criminal asylum at Parkhurst, 2 to Broadmoor asylum, 3 to county or borough asylums, and 3 remained in the prison infirmary at the end of the year.

"The average length of the last sentences for which these unfortunates were committed was seven years' penal servitude each. That their mental condition was not temporary but permanent may be gathered from their educational attainments, for 12 had no education at all, 18 were only in Standard I, 29 in Standard II, 15 in Standard III, and 12 others were of poor education."

The statement that the average length of the last sentences of these unfortunates was seven years' penal servitude is appalling. It ought to astound us! But no one seems to care. Penal servitude is good enough for them. Perhaps it is! But it ought to be called by another name, and legally signify the inmates to be "patients," not criminals. Let us visit a prison where we shall find a sufficient number of prisoners to enable us to form an idea as to their physical and mental condition.

Come, then, on Sunday morning into a famous prison that long stood as a model to the world. We are going to morning service, when we shall have an opportunity of seeing face to face eight hundred male prisoners. But before we enter the chapel, let us walk round the hospital and see those who are on the sick list.

One look as we enter the ward convinced us that some are lying there whose only chance of freedom is through the gates of death.

In yonder corner lies a young man of twenty-one years; the governor tells us that he is friendless, homeless, and a hopeless consumptive. He says, "We would have sent him out, but he has nowhere to go, for he does not know his parish, so he must lie here till he dies, unless his sentence expires first."

We speak to the young man a few kindly words, but he turns his face from us, and of his history we learn nothing.

On another bed we find an old man whose days also will be short; of his history we learn much, for he has spent a great deal of his life in prison, and now, aged, feeble and broken, there is nothing before him but death or continued imprisonment. We pass by other beds on which prisoners not so hopeless in health are lying. We see what is the matter with most of them: they are not strong enough for ordinary prison work, or indeed for any kind of vigorous labour. So they remain in prison well tended in the hospital. But some of them pass into freedom without the slightest ability or chance of getting a living otherwise than by begging or stealing.

What strikes us most about the inmates of the prison hospital is the certainty that many of the prisoners have not sufficient health and strength to enable them to be useful citizens.

So we pass through the hospital into the chapel, and find eight hundred prisoners before us. The organ plays, the morning service is read by the chaplain; the prisoners sing, and as they sing there is such a volume of sound that we cannot fail to be touched with it.

We enter the pulpit, and as we stand and look down upon that sea of upturned faces, we see a sight that is not likely to be forgotten. There, in front of us, right underneath the pulpit, are rows of young men under twenty-two years of age; we look at them; they are all clad in khaki, and we take a mental sketch of them.

One or two among them are finely developed young men, but the great bulk we see are small in stature and weak in body. Some of them have a hopeless expression of countenance that tells us of moral and mental weakness.

We note that most of them can have had but little chance in life, and that their physical or mental infirmities come from no fault of their own. They have all been to school; they have started in life, if it can be called starting, as errand boys, paper sellers in the streets, or as street merchants of some description. They have grown into early manhood, but they have not increased in wisdom or stature. They have learned no occupation, trade or handicraft; they have passed from school age to early manhood without discipline, decent homes or technical training.

When at liberty their homes are lodging-houses or even less desirable places. So they pass from the streets to the police, from police-courts to prison, with positive regularity.

They behave themselves in prison, they obey orders, they do the bit of work that is required of them, they eat the food, and they sleep interminable hours away.

At the back of the young men we see row after row of older men, and their khaki clothing and broad arrows produce a strange impression upon us; but what impresses us most is the facial and physical appearance of the prisoners.

Cripples are there, twisted bodies are there, one-armed men are there, and blind men are there. Here and there we see a healthy man, with vigour and strength written on his face; but the great mass of faces strikes us with dismay, and we feel at once that most of them are handicapped in life, and demand pity rather than vengeance.

We know that they are not as other men, and we realise that their afflictions more than their sins are responsible for their presence in that doleful assembly.

Yet some of them are clever in crime, and many of them persistent in wrong-doing, but their afflictions were neglected in days when those afflictions should have been a passport to the pity and care of the community.

We see men who have grown old in different prisons, and we know that position in social and industrial life is impossible for them.

We see a number whom it is evident are not mentally responsible, for whom there is no place but the workhouse or prison; yet we realise that, old as they are, the day of liberty must come once more, and they will be free to starve or steal!

We know that there are some epileptics among them, and that their dread complaint has caused them to commit acts of violence.

We see among them men of education that have made war upon society. Drunkards, too, are there, and we know that their overmastering passion will demand gratification when once again the opportunity of indulging in its presented to them. So we look at this strange mass of humanity, and as we look a mist comes over our eyes, and we feel a choking sensation in our throats.

But we look again, and see that few throughout this great assembly show any sense of sorrow or shame. As we speak to them of hope, gladness, of manliness, and of the dignity of life, we feel that we are preaching to an east wind. Come round the same prison with me on a week-day; in one part we find a number of men seated about six feet from each other making baskets; warders are placed on pedestals here and there to keep oversight.

We walk past them, and notice their slow movements and see hopelessness written all over them. They are working "in association," they are under "observation," which, the governor tells us, means that they are suspected of either madness or mental deficiency.

As we look at them we are quite satisfied that this suspicion is true, and that, if not absolutely mad, they are mentally deficient.

If absolute madness be detected, they will be sent to asylums. If feeble-mindedness be proved, they will again be set at liberty. Their names will be placed on a list, and they will be declared "unfit for prison discipline," but nothing more will be done. They will be discharged to prowl about in the underworld, to commit other criminal acts and to be returned again and again to prison, to live out hopeless lives.

And there is another cause, almost as prolific in producing a prison population. For while the State has been, and still is, ready to thrust afflicted youth into prison, it has been, and still is, equally ready to thrust into prison the half-educated, half-fed, and half-employed young people who break its laws or by-laws. It is true that the State in its irony allows them the option of a fine; but the law might as well ask the youths of the underworld to pay ten pounds as ask them to pay ten shillings; nor can they procure all at once the smaller sum, so to prison hundreds of lads are sent.

Does it ever occur to our esteemed authorities that this is a most dangerous procedure! What good can possibly come either to the State or to the youthful offender?

What are the offences of these boys? Disorder in the streets, loitering at railway stations, playing a game of chance called "pitch and toss," of which I have something to say in another chapter, gambling with a penny pack of cards, playing tip-cat, kicking a football, made of old newspapers maybe, playing cricket, throwing stones, using a catapult, bathing in a canal, and a hundred similar things are all deemed worthy of imprisonment, if committed by the youngsters of the world below the line.

Thousands of lads have had their first experience of prison for trumpery offences that are natural to the boys of the poor. But a first experience of prison is to them a pleasant surprise. They are astonished to find that prison is not "half a bad place." They do not object to going there again, not they! Why? Because the conditions of prison life are better, as they need to be, than the conditions of their own homes. The food is better, the lodging is better, the bed is decidedly better, and as to the work, why, they have none worthy of the name to do. They lose nothing but their liberty, and they can stand that for a week or two, what matters!

Well, something does matter, for they lose three other things of great moment to them if they only knew; but they don't know, and our authorities evidently consider these three things of no moment. What do they lose? First, their fear of prison; secondly, their little bit of character; thirdly, their work, if they have any. What eventuates? Idleness, hooliganism and repeated imprisonments for petty crime, until something more serious happens, and then longer sentences. Such is the progress of hundreds whom statisticians love to call "recidivists."

Am I wrong when I say that the State has been too ready, too prompt in sending the youths of the ignorant poor to prison? Am I wrong in saying that the State has been playing its "trump ace" too soon, and that it ought to have kept imprisonment up its sleeve a little longer? These lads, having been in prison, know, and their companions know, too, the worst that can happen to them when they commit real crime. Prison has done its worst, and it cannot hurt them.

If prisons there must be, am I wrong in contending that they should be reserved for the perpetrators of real and serious crime; and that the punishment, if there is to be punishment, should be certain, dignified and severe, educational and reformative? At present it includes none of these qualities.

To such a length has the imprisonment of youths for trumpery offences gone, not only in London, but throughout the country, that visiting justices of my acquaintance have spent a great deal of money in part paying the fines of youths imprisoned under such conditions, that they might be released at once. Here we have a curious state of affairs, magistrates generally committing youths to prison in default for trumpery offences, and other magistrates searching prisons for imprisoned youths, paying their fines, setting them free, and sending on full details to the Home Secretary.

It would be interesting to know how many "cases" of this kind have been reported to the Home Secretary during the last few years. Time after time the governors of our prisons have called attention to this evil in their annual reports. They know perfectly well the disaster that attends the needless imprisonment of boys, and it worries them. They treat the boys very kindly, all honour to them! But even kindness to young prisoners has its dangers, and every governor is able to tell of the constant return of youthful prisoners.

I do not like the "birch" or corporal punishment at all. I do not advocate it, but I am certain that the demoralising effect of a few' days' imprisonment is far in excess of the demoralisation that follows a reasonable application of the birch.

But the birch cannot be applied to lads over fourteen years of age, so it would be well to abolish it altogether, except in special cases, and for these the age might with advantage be extended. And, after all, imprisonment itself is physical punishment and a continued assault upon the body. But why imprison at all for such cases? We talk about imprisonment for debt; this is imprisonment for debt with a vengeance. Look! two lads are charged with one offence or two similar offences; one boy is from the upperworld, the other from below the line. The same magistrate fines the two boys an equal amount; the one boy pays, or his friends pay; but the other goes of a certainty to prison. Is it not absurd! rather, is it not unjust?

But whether it is absurd or unjust the result is certain—mathematically certain—in the development of a prison population.

During my police-court days I have seen hundreds of youths sitting crying in their cells consumed with fear, waiting their first experience of prison; I have seen their terror when first entering the prison van, and I know that when entering the prison portals their terror increased. But it soon vanished, for I have never seen boys cry, or show any signs of fear when going to prison for the second time. The reason for this I have already given: "fear of the unknown" has been removed. This fear may not be a very noble characteristic, but it is part of us, and it has a useful place, especially where penalties are likely to be incurred.

For many years I have been protesting against this needless imprisonment of youths, and now it has become part of my duty to visit prisons and to talk to youthful prisoners, I see the wholesale evil that attends this method of dealing with youthful offenders. And the same evils attend, though to perhaps a less degree, the prompt imprisonment of adults, who are unable to pay forthwith fines that have been imposed upon them.

It is always the poor, the very poor, the people below the line that suffer in this direction. Doubtless they merit some correction, and the magistrates consider that fines of ten shillings are appropriate, but then they thoughtlessly add "or seven days."

Think of the folly of it! because a man cannot pay a few shillings down, the State conveys him to prison and puts the community to the very considerable expense of keeping him. The law has fined him, but he cannot pay then, so the law turns round and fines the community.

What sense, decency, or profit can there possibly be in committing women to prison, even for drunkenness, for three, five or seven days? How can it profit either the State or the woman? It only serves to familiarise her with prison.

I could laugh at it, were it not so serious. Just look at this absurdity! A woman gets drunk on Thursday, she is charged on Friday. "Five shillings, or three days!" On Friday afternoon she enters prison, for the clerk has made out a "commitment," and the gaoler has handed her into the prison van. Her "commitment" is handed to the prison authorities; it is tabulated, so is she; but at nine o'clock next morning she is discharged from prison, for the law reckons every part of a day to be a complete day; and the law also says that there must be no discharge from prison on a Sunday, and to keep her till Monday would be illegal, for it would be "four days." How small, how disastrous, and how expensive it is!

If offenders, young or old, must be punished, let them be punished decently. If they ought to be sent to prison, to prison send them. But if their petty offences can be expunged by the payment of a few shillings, why not give them a little time to pay those fines? Such a course would stop for ever the miserable, deadly round of short expensive imprisonments. I have approached succeeding Home Secretaries upon this matter till I am tired; succeeding Home Secretaries have sent memorandums and recommendations to courts of summary jurisdiction till, I expect, they are tired, for generally they have had no effect in mitigating the evil.

Magistrates have the power to grant time for the payment of fines, but it is optional, not imperative. It is high time for a change, and surely it will come, for the absurdity cannot continue.

Surely every English man and woman who possesses a settled home ought to have, and must have, the legal right of a few days' grace in which to pay his or her fine. And every youthful offender ought to have the same right, also, even if he paid by instalments.

But at present it is so much easier, and therefore so much better, to thrust the underworld, youthful and adult, into prison and have done with them, than it is to pursue a sane but a little bit troublesome method that would keep thousands of the poor from ever entering prison.

XIII

Unemployed
and Unemployable

My life has been one of activity; from an early age I have known what it was to be constantly at work. To have the certainty of regular work, and to have the discipline of constant duty, seem to me an ideal state for mind and body. Labour, we are sometimes told, is one of God's chastisements upon a fallen race; I believe it to be one of our choicest blessings. I can conceive only one greater tragedy than the man who has nothing to do, and that is the man who, earnestly longing for work, seeks it day by day, and fails to find it.

Imagine his position, and imagine also, if you possibly can, the great qualities that are demanded if such a man is to go through a lengthened period of unemployment without losing his dignity, his manhood and his desire for work.

I can tell at a glance the man who has had this experience. There is something about his face that proclaims his hopelessness, the very poise of his body and his peculiar measured step tell that his heart is utterly unexpectant. To-morrow morning, and every morning, thousands of men will rise early, even before the sun, and set out on their weary tramp and hopeless search for work. To-morrow morning, and every morning, thousands of men will be waiting at various dock-gates for a chance of obtaining a few hours' hard work. And while these wait, others tramp, seeking and asking for work.

Wives may be ill at home, children may be wanting food and clothing, but every day thousands of husbands set out on the interminable search for work, and every day return disappointed. Small wonder that some of them descend to a lower grade and in addition to being unemployed, become unemployable.

Look at those thousands of men clamouring daily at our dock-gates; about one-half of them will obtain a few hours' hard work, but the other half will go hopeless away. They will gather some courage during the night, for the next morning they will find their way to, and be knocking once more at, the same dock-gates. It takes sterling qualities to endure this life, and there can be no greater hero than the man who goes through it and still retains manhood.

But it would be more than a miracle if tens of thousands of men could live this life without many of them becoming wastrels, for it is certain that a life of unemployment is dangerous to manhood, to character and health.

As a matter of fact the ranks of the utterly submerged are being constantly recruited from the ranks of those who have but casual work. During winter the existence of the unemployed is more amply demonstrated, for then we are called upon to witness the most depressing of all London's sights, a parade of the unemployed. I never see one without experiencing strange and mixed emotions. Let me picture a parade, for where I live they are numerous, and at least once a week one will pass my window.

I hear the doleful strains of a tin whistle accompanied with a rub-a-dub-dub of a kettledrum that has known its best days, and whose sound is as doleful as that of the whistle. I know what is coming, and, though I have seen it many times, it has still a fascination for me, so I stand at my window and watch. I see two men carrying a dilapidated banner, on which is inscribed two words, "The Unemployed." The man with the tin whistle and the man with the drum follow the banner, and behind them is a company of men marching four abreast. Two policemen on the pavement keep pace with the head of the procession, and two others perform a similar duty at the end of it.

On the pavement are a number of men with collecting boxes, ready to receive any contribution that charitably inclined people may bestow. They do not knock at any door, but they stand for a moment and rattle their boxes in front of every window.

The sound of the whistle and the drum, and the rattle of boxes is, in all conscience, depressing enough, but one glimpse at the men is infinitely more so.

Most of them are below the average height and bulk. Their hands are in their trousers pockets, their shoulders are up, but their heads are bent downwards as if they were half ashamed of their job. A peculiar slouching gait is characteristic of the whole company, and I look in vain for a firm step, an upright carriage, and for some signs of alert manhood. As they pass slowly by I see that some are old, but I also see that the majority of them are comparatively young, and that many of them cannot be more than thirty years of age. But whether young or old, I am conscious of the fact that few of them are possessed of strength, ability and grit. There are no artisans or craftsmen among them, and stalwart labourers are not in evidence.

Pitiful as the procession is, I know that it does not represent the genuine and struggling unemployed. They pass slowly by and go from street to street. So they will parade throughout the livelong day. The police will accompany them, and will see them disbanded when the evening closes in. The boxes will be emptied, the contents tabulated, and a pro rata division will be made, after which the processionists will go home and remain unemployed till the next weekly parade comes round.

Unemployable! yes, but so much the greater pity; and so much more difficult the problem, for they represent a very large class, and it is to be feared a growing class of the manhood of London's underworld.

We cannot blame them for their physical inferiority, nor for their lack of ability and grit. To expect them to exhibit great qualities would be absurd. They are what they are, and a wise country would ponder the causes that lead to such decadent manhood. During my prison lectures I have been frequently struck with the mean size and appearance of the prisoners under twenty-two years of age, who are so numerous in our London prisons. From many conversations with them I have learned that lack of physical strength means also lack of mental and moral strength, and lack of honest aspiration, too! I am confirmed in this judgment by a statement that appeared in the annual report of the Prison Commissioners, who state that some years ago they adapted the plan in Pentonville prison of weighing and measuring all the prisoners under the age of twenty-two.

The result I will tell in their own words: "As a class they are two-and-a-half inches below the average height of the general youthful population of the same age, and weigh approximately fourteen pounds less."

Here, then, we have an official proof of physical decadence, and of its connection with prison life. For these young men, so continuously in prison, grow into what should be manhood without any desire or qualification for robust industrial life.

I never speak to them without feeling a deep pity. But as it is my business to interest them, I try to learn something from them in return, as the following illustration will show.

I had been giving a course of lectures on industrial life to the young prisoners in Wormwood Scrubbs, who numbered over three hundred. On my last visit I interrogated them as follows—

"Stand up those of you that have had regular or continuous work." None of them stood up! "Stand up those of you who have been apprentices." None of them stood up! "Stand up those of you who sold papers in the street before you left school." Twenty-five responded! "How many sold other things in the streets before leaving school?" Thirty! Seventeen others sold papers after leaving school, and thirty-eight sold various articles. Altogether I found that nearly two hundred had been in street occupations.

To my final question: "How many of you have met me in other prisons?" Thirty-five stood up! I give these particulars because I think my readers will realise the bearing they have on unemployment.

Surely it is obvious that if we continue to have a growing number of physically inferior young men, who acquire no technical skill and have not the slightest industrial training, that we shall continue to have an increasing number of unemployed unemployables.

XIV

Suggestions

I propose in this last chapter to make some suggestions, which, I venture to hope, will be found worthy of consideration and adoption.

The causes of so much misery, suffering and poverty in a rich and self-governing country are numerous; and every cause needs a separate consideration and remedy.

There is no royal road by which the underworld people can ascend to the upperworld; there can be no specific for healing all the sores from which humanity suffers.

Our complex civilisation, our industrial methods, our strange social system, combined with the varied characteristics mental and physical of individuals, make social salvation for the mass difficult and quite impossible for many.

I shall have written with very little effect if I have not shown what some of these individual characteristics are. They are strange, powerful and extraordinary. So very mixed, even in one individual, that while sometimes they inspire hope, at others they provoke despair.

If we couple the difficulties of individual character with the social, industrial and economic difficulties, we see at once how great the problem is.

We must admit, and we ought frankly to admit the truth, and to face it, that there exists a very large army of people that cannot be socially saved. What is more important, they do not want to be saved, and will not be saved if they can avoid it. Their great desire is to be left alone, to be allowed to live where and how they like.

For these people there must be, there will be, and at no far distant date, detention, segregation and classification. We must let them quietly die out, for it is not only folly, but suicidal folly to allow them to continue and to perpetuate.

But we are often told that "Heaven helps those who help themselves"; in fact, we have been told it so often that we have come to believe it, and, what is worse, we religiously or irreligiously act upon it when dealing with those below the line.

If any serious attempt is ever made to lessen the number of the homeless and destitute, if that attempt is to have any chance of success, it will, I am sure, be necessary to make an alteration in the adage and a reversal of our present methods.

If the adage ran, "Heaven helps those who cannot help themselves," and if we all placed ourselves on the side of Heaven, the present abominable and distressing state of affairs would not endure for a month,

Now I charge it upon the State and local authorities that they avoid their responsibilities to those who most sorely need their help, and who, too, have the greatest claim upon their pity and protecting care. Sometimes those claims are dimly recognised, and half-hearted efforts are made to care for the unfortunate for a short space of time, and to protect them for a limited period.

But these attempts only serve to show the futility of the efforts, for the unfortunates are released from protective care at the very time when care and protection should become more effectual and permanent.

It is comforting to know that we have in London special schools for afflicted or defective children. Day by day hundreds of children are taken to these schools, where genuine efforts are made to instruct them and to develop their limited powers. But eight hundred children leave these schools every year; in five years four thousand afflicted children leave these schools. Leave the schools to live in the underworld of London, and leave, too, just at the age when protection is urgently needed. For adolescence brings new passions that need either control or prohibition.

I want my reader's imagination to dwell for a moment on these four thousand defectives that leave our special schools every five years; I want them to ask themselves what becomes of these children, and to remember that what holds good with London's special schools, holds good with regard to all other special schools our country over.

These young people grow into manhood and womanhood without the possibility of growing in wisdom or skill. Few, very few of them, have the slightest chance of becoming self-reliant or self-supporting; ultimately they form a not inconsiderable proportion of the hopeless.

Philanthropic societies receive some of them, workhouses receive others, but these institutions have not, nor do they wish to have, any power of permanent detention, the cost would be too great. Sooner or later the greater part of them become a costly burden upon the community, and an eyesore to humanity. Many of them live nomadic lives, and make occasional use of workhouses and similar institutions when the weather is bad, after which they return to their uncontrolled existence. Feeble-minded and defective women return again and again to the maternity wards to deposit other burdens upon the ratepayers and to add to the number of their kind.

But the nation has begun to realise this costly absurdity of leaving this army of irresponsibles in possession of uncontrolled liberty. The Royal Commission on the Care and Control of the Feeble-minded, after sitting for four years, has made its report. This report is a terrible document and an awful indictment of our neglect.

The commissioners tell us that on January 1st, 1906, there were in England and Wales 149,628 idiots, imbeciles, and feeble-minded; in addition there were on the same date 121,079 persons suffering from some kind of insanity or dementia. So that the total number of those who came within the scope of the inquiry was no less than 271,607, or 1 in every 120 of the whole population.

Of the persons suffering from mental defect, i.e. feeble-minded, imbeciles, etc., one-third were supported entirely at the public cost in workhouses, asylums, prisons, etc.

The report does not tell us much about the remaining two-thirds; but those of us who have experience know only too well what becomes of them, and are painfully acquainted with the hopelessness of their lives.

Here, then, is my first suggestion—a national plan for the permanent detention, segregation and control of all persons who are indisputably feeble-minded. Surely this must be the duty of the State, for it is impossible that philanthropic societies can deal permanently with them.

We must catch them young; we must make them happy, for they have capabilities for childlike happiness, and we must make their lives as useful as possible. But we must no longer allow them the curse of uncontrolled liberty.

Again, no boy should be discharged from reformatory or industrial schools as "unfit for training" unless passed on to some institution suitable to his age and condition. If we have no such institutions, as of course we have not, then the State must provide them. And the magistrates must have the power to commit boys and girls who are charged before them to suitable industrial schools or reformatories as freely, as certainly, as unquestioned, and as definitely as they now commit them to prison.

At present magistrates have not this power, for though, as a matter of course, these institutions receive numbers of boys and girls from police-courts, the institutions have the power to Refuse, to grant "licences" or to "discharge." So it happens that the meshes of the net are large enough to allow those that ought to be detained to go free.

No one can possibly doubt that a provision of this character would largely diminish the number of those that become homeless vagrants.

But I proceed to my second suggestion—the detention and segregation of all professional tramps. If it is intolerable that an army of poor afflicted human beings should live homeless and nomadic lives, it is still more intolerable that an army of men and women who are not deficient in intelligence, and who are possessed of fairly healthy bodies should, in these days, be allowed to live as our professional tramps live.

I have already spoken of the fascination attached to a life of irresponsible liberty. The wind on the heath, the field and meadow glistening with dew or sparkling with flowers, the singing of the bird, the joy of life, and no rent day coming round, who would not be a tramp! Perhaps our professional tramps think nothing of these things, for to eat, to sleep, to be free of work, to be uncontrolled, to have no anxieties, save the gratification of animal demands and animal passions, is the perfection of life for thousands of our fellow men and women.

Is this kind of life to be permitted? Every sensible person will surely say that it ought not to be permitted. Yet the number of people who attach themselves to this life continually increases, for year by year the prison commissioners tell us that the number of persons imprisoned for vagrancy, sleeping out, indecency, etc., continues to increase, and that short terms of imprisonment only serve as periods of recuperation for them, for in prison they are healed of their sores and cleansed from their vermin.

With every decent fellow who tramps in search of work we must have the greatest sympathy, but for professional tramps we must provide very simply. Most of these men, women and children find their way into prison, workhouses and casual wards at some time or other. When the man gets into prison, the woman and children go into the nearest workhouse. When the man is released from prison he finds the woman and children waiting for him, and away they go refreshed and cleansed by prison and workhouse treatment.

We must stop for ever this costly and disastrous course of life. How? By establishing in every county and under county authorities, or, if necessary, by a combination of counties, special colonies for vagrants, one for males and another for females. Every vagrant who could not give proof that he had some definite object in tramping must be committed to these colonies and detained, till such time as definite occupation or home be found for him.

Here they should live and work, practically earning their food and clothing; their lives should be made clean and decent, and certainly economical. For these colonies there must be of course State aid.

The children must be adopted by the board of guardians or education authorities and trained in small homes outside the workhouse gates this should be compulsory.

These two plans would certainly clear away the worst and most hopeless tribes of nomads, and though for a short time they would impose considerable pecuniary obligations upon us, yet we should profit even financially in the near future, and, best of all, should prevent a second generation arising to fill the place of those detained.

The same methods should be adopted with the wretched mass of humanity that crowds nightly on the Thames Embankment. Philanthropy is worse than useless with the great majority of these people. Hot soup in the small hours of a cold morning is doubtless comforting to them, and if the night is wet, foggy, etc., a cover for a few hours is doubtless a luxury. They drink the soup, they take advantage of the cover, and go away, to return at night for more soup and still another cover. Oh, the folly of it all!

We must have shelters for them, but the County Council must provide them. Large, clean and healthy places into which, night by night, the human derelicts from the streets should be taken by special police.

But there should be no release with the morning light, but detention while full inquiries are made regarding them. Friends would doubtless come forward to help many, but the remainder should be classified according to age and physical and mental condition, and released only when some satisfactory place or occupation is forthcoming for them.

The nightly condition of the Embankment is not only disgraceful, but it is dangerous to the health and wellbeing of the community.

It is almost inconceivable that we should allow those parts of London which are specially adapted for the convenience of the public to be monopolised by a mass of diseased and unclean humanity. If we would but act sensibly with these classes, I am sure we could then deal in an effectual manner with that portion of the nomads for whom there is hope.

If the vast amount of money that is poured out in the vain effort to help those whom it is impossible to help was devoted to those that are helpable, the difficulty would be solved,

So I would suggest, and it is no new suggestion, that all philanthropic societies that deal with the submerged should unite and co-ordinate with the authorities. That private individuals who have money, time or ability at their command should unite with them. That one great all-embracing organisation, empowered and aided by the State, should be formed, to which the man, woman or family that is overtaken or overwhelmed by misfortune could turn in time of their need with the assurance that their needs would be sympathetically considered and their requirements wisely attended to.

An organisation of this description would prevent tens of thousands from becoming vagrants, and a world of misery and unspeakable squalor would be prevented.

The recent Report on the Poor Law foreshadows an effort of this description, and in Germany this method is tried with undoubted success.

Some day we shall try it, but that day will not come till we have realised how futile, how expensive our present methods are. The Poor Law system needs recasting. Charity must be divorced from religion. Philanthropic and semi-religious organisations must be separated from their commercial instincts and commercial greed. The workhouse, the prison, the Church Army and the Salvation Army's shelters and labour homes must no longer form the circle round which so many hopelessly wander.

No man or set of men must be considered the saviour of the poor, and though much knowledge will be required, it perhaps will be well not to have too much.

Above all, the desire to prevent, rather than the desire to restore, must be the aim of the organisation which should embrace every parish in our land.

Finally, and in a few words, my methods would be detention and protective care for the afflicted or defective, detention and segregation for the tramps, and a great charitable State-aided organisation to deal with the unfortunate.

Tramps we shall continue to have, but there need be nothing degrading about them, if only the professional element can be eliminated.

Labour exchanges are doing a splendid work for the genuine working man whose labour must often be migratory. But every labour exchange should have its clean lodging-house, in which the decent fellows who want work, and are fitted for work, may stay for a night, and thus avoid the contamination attending the common lodging-houses or the degradation and detention attending casual wards.

There exists, I am sure, great possibilities for good in labour exchanges, if, and if only, their services can be devoted to the genuinely unemployed.

Already I have said they are doing much, and one of the most useful things they do is the advancement of rail-fares to men when work is obtained at a distance. A development in this direction will do much to end the disasters that attend decent fellows when they go on tramp. Migratory labour is unfortunately an absolute necessity, for our industrial and commercial life demand it, and almost depend upon it. The men who supply that want are quite as useful citizens as the men who have permanent and settled work. But their lives are subject to many dangers, temptations, and privations from which they ought to be delivered.

The more I reflect upon the present methods for dealing with professional tramps, the more I am persuaded that these methods are foolish and extravagant. But the more I reflect on the life of the genuinely unemployed that earnestly desire work and are compelled to tramp in search of it, the more I am persuaded that such life is attended by many dangers. The probability being that if the tramp and search be often repeated or long-continued, the desire for, and the ability to undergo, regular work will disappear.

But physical and mental inferiority, together with the absence of moral purpose, have a great deal to say with regard to the number of our unemployed.

If you ask me the source of this stunted manhood, I point you to the narrow streets of the underworld. Thence they issue, and thence alone.

Do you ask the cause? The causes are many! First and foremost stands that all-pervading cause—the housing of the poor. Who can enumerate the thousands that have breathed the fetid air of the miserable dwelling-places in our slums? Who dare picture how they live and sleep, as they lie, unripe sex with sex, for mutual taint? I dare not, and if I did no publisher could print it.

Who dare describe the life of a mother-wife, whose husband and children have become dependent upon her earnings! I dare not! Who dare describe the exact life and doings of four families living in a little house intended for one family? Who can describe the life, speech, actions and atmosphere of such places? I cannot, for the task would be too disgusting!

For tens of thousands of people are allowed, or compelled, to live and die under those conditions. How can vigorous manhood or pure womanhood come out of them? Ought we to expect, have we any right to expect, manhood and womanhood born and bred under such conditions to be other than blighted?

Whether we expect it or not matters but little, for we have this mass of blighted humanity with us, and, like an old man of the sea, it is a burden upon our back, a burden that is not easily got rid of.

What are we doing with this burden in the present? How are we going to prevent it in the future? are two serious questions that must be answered, and quickly, too, or something worse will happen to us.

The authorities must see to it at once that children shall have as much air and breathing space in their homes by night as they have in the schools by day.

What sense can there be in demanding and compelling a certain amount of air space in places where children are detained for five and a half hours, and then allow those children to stew in apologies for rooms, where the atmosphere is vile beyond description, and where they are crowded indiscriminately for the remaining hours?

This is the question of the day and the hour. Drink, foreign invasion, the House of Lords or the House of Commons, Tariff Reform or Free Trade, none of these questions, no, nor the whole lot of them combined, compare for one moment in importance with this one awful question.

Give the poor good airy housing at a reasonable rent, and half the difficulties against which our nation runs its thick head would disappear. Hospitals and prisons would disappear too as if by magic, for it is to these places that the smitten manhood finds its way.

I know it is a big question! But it is a question that has got to be solved, and in solving it some of our famous and cherished notions will have to go. Every house, no matter to whom it belongs, or who holds the lease, who lets or sub-lets, every inhabited house must be licensed by the local authorities for a certain number of inmates, so many and no more; a maximum, but no minimum.

Local authorities even now have great powers concerning construction, drains, etc. Let them now be empowered to make stringent rules about habitations other than their municipal houses. The piggeries misnamed lodging-houses, the common shelters, etc., are inspected and licensed for a certain number of inmates; it is high time that this was done with the wretched houses in which the poor live.

Oh, the irony of it! Idle tramps must not be crowded, but the children of the poor may be crowded to suffocation. This must surely stop; if not, it will stop us! Again I say, that local authorities must have the power to decide the number of inhabitants that any house shall accommodate, and license it accordingly, and of course have legal power to enforce their decision.

The time has come for a thorough investigation. I would have every room in every house visited by properly appointed officers. I would have every detail as to size of room, number of persons and children, rent paid, etc., etc.; I would have its conditions and fitness for human habitation inquired into and reported upon.

I would miss no house, I would excuse none. A standard should be set as to the condition and position of every house, and the number it might be allowed to accommodate. This would bring many dark things into the light of day, and I am afraid the reputation of many respectable people would suffer, and their pockets too, although they tell us that they "have but a life-interest" in the pestiferous places. But if we drive people out of these places, where will they go?

Well, out they must go! and it is certain that there is at present no place for them!

Places must be prepared for them, and local authorities must prepare them. Let them address themselves to this matter and no longer shirk their duty with regard to the housing of the poor. Let them stop for ever the miserable pretence of housing the poor that they at present pursue. For be it known that they house "respectable" people only, those that have limited families and can pay a high rental.

If local authorities cannot do it, then the State must step in and help them, for it must be done. It seems little use waiting for private speculation or philanthropic trusts to show us the way in this matter, for both want and expect too high an interest for their outlay. But a good return will assuredly be forthcoming if the evil be tackled in a sensible way.

Let no one be downhearted about new schemes for housing the poor not paying! Why, everything connected with the poor from the cradle to the grave is a source of good profit to some one, if not to themselves.

Let a housing plan be big enough and simple enough, and I am certain that it will pay even when it provides for the very poor. But old ideals will have to be forsaken and new ones substituted.

I have for many years considered this question very deeply, and from the side of the very poor. I think that I know how the difficulty can be met, and I am prepared to place my suggestions for housing the poor before any responsible person or authority who would care to consider the matter.

Perhaps it is due to the public to say here that one of the greatest sorrows of my life was my inability to make good a scheme that a rich friend and myself formulated some years ago. This failure was due to the serious illness of my friend, and I hope that it will yet materialise.

But, in addition to the housing, there are other matters which affect the vigour and virility of the poor. School days must be extended till the age of sixteen. Municipal playgrounds open in the evening must be established. If boys and girls are kept at school till sixteen, older and weaker people will be able to get work which these boys have, but ought not to have. The nation demands a vigorous manhood, but the nation cannot have it without some sacrifice, which means doing without child labour, for child labour is the destruction of virile manhood.

Emigration is often looked upon as the great specific. But the multiplication of agencies for exporting the young, the healthy, and the strong to the colonies causes me some alarm. For emigration as at present conducted certainly does not lessen the number of the unfit and the helpless.

It must be apparent to any one who thinks seriously upon this matter that a continuance of the present methods is bound to entail disastrous consequences, and to promote racial decay at home. The problem of the degenerates, the physical and mental weaklings is already a pressing national question. But serious as the question is at the present moment, it is but light in its intensity compared with what it must be in the near future, unless we change our methods. One fact ought to be definitely understood and seriously pondered, and it is this: no emigration agency, no board of guardians, no church organisation and no human salvage organisation emigrates or assists to emigrate young people of either sex who cannot pass a severe medical examination and be declared mentally and physically sound. This demands serious thought; for the puny, the weak and the unfit are ineligible; our colonies will have none of them, and perhaps our colonies are wise, so the unfit remain at home to be our despair and affliction.

But our colonies demand not only physical and mental health, but moral health also, for boys and girls from reformatory and industrial schools are not acceptable; though the training given in these institutions ought to make the young people valuable assets in a new country.

The serious fact that only the best are exported and that all the afflicted and the weak remain at home is, I say, worthy of profound attention.

Thousands of healthy working men with a little money and abundant grit emigrate of their own choice and endeavour. Fine fellows they generally are, and good fortune attends them! Thousands of others with no money but plenty of strength are assisted "out," and they are equally good, while thousands of healthy young women are assisted "out" also. All through the piece the strong and healthy leave our shores, and the weaklings are left at home.

It is always with mixed feelings that I read of boys and girls being sent to Canada, for while I feel hopeful regarding their future, I know that the matter does not end with them; for I appreciate some of the evils that result to the old country from the method of selection.

Emigration, then, as at present conducted, is no cure for the evil it is supposed to remedy. Nay, it increases the evil, for it secures to our country an ever-increasing number of those who are absolutely unfitted to fulfil the duties of citizenship.

Yet emigration might be a beneficent thing if it were wisely conducted on a comprehensive basis, which should include a fair proportion of those that are now excluded because of their unfitness.

Are we to go on far ever with our present method of dealing with those who have been denied wisdom and stature? Who are what they are, but whose disabilities cannot be charged upon themselves, and for whom there is no place other than prison or workhouse?

Yet many of them have wits, if not brains, and are clever in little ways of their own. At home we refuse them the advantages that are solicitously pressed upon their bigger and stronger brothers. Abroad every door is locked against them. What are they to do? The Army and Navy will have none of them! and industrial life has no place for them. So prison, workhouse and common lodging-houses are their only homes.

Wise emigration methods would include many of them, and decent fellows they would make if given a chance. Oxygen and new environment, with plenty of food, etc., would make an alteration in their physique, and regular work would prove their salvation. But this matter should, and must be, undertaken by the State, for philanthropy cannot deal with it; and when the State does undertake it, consequences unthought-of will follow, for the State will be able to close one-half of its prisons.

It is the helplessness of weaklings that provides the State with more than half its prisoners. Is it impossible, I would ask, for a Government like ours, with all its resources of wealth, power and influence to devise and carry out some large scheme of emigration? If colonial governments wisely refuse our inferior youths, is it not unwise for our own Government to neglect them?

In the British Empire is there no idle land that calls for men and culture? Here we in England have thousands of young fellows who, because of their helplessness, are living lives of idleness and wrongdoing.

Time after time these young men find their way into prison, and every short sentence they undergo sends them back to liberty more hopeless and helpless. Many of them are not bad fellows; they have some qualities that are estimable, but they are undisciplined and helpless. Not all the discharged prisoners' aid societies in the land, even with Government assistance, can procure reasonable and progressive employment for them.

The thought of thousands of young men, not criminals, spending their lives in a senseless and purposeless round of short imprisonments, simply because they are not quite as big and as strong as their fellows, fills me with wonder and dismay, for I can estimate some of the consequences that result.

Is it impossible, I would ask, for our Government to take up this matter in a really great way? Can no arrangement be made with our colonies for the reception and training of these young fellows? Probably not so long as the colonies can secure an abundance of better human material. But has a bona-fide effort been made in this direction? I much doubt it since the days of transportation.

Is it not possible for our Government to obtain somewhere in the whole of its empire a sufficiency of suitable land, to which the best of them may be transplanted, and on which they may be trained for useful service and continuous work?

Is it not possible to develop the family system for them, and secure a sufficient number of house fathers and mothers to care for them in a domestic way, leaving their physical and industrial training to others? Very few know these young fellows better than myself, and I am bold enough to say that under such conditions the majority of them would prove useful men.

Surely a plan of this description would be infinitely better than continued imprisonments for miserable offences, and much less expensive, too!

I am very anxious to emphasise this point. The extent of our prison population depends upon the treatment these young men receive at the hands of the State.

So long as the present treatment prevails, so long will the State be assured of a permanent prison population.

But the evil does not end with the continuance and expense of prison. The army of the unfit is perpetually increased by this procedure. Very few of these young men—I think I may say with safety, none of them—after three or four convictions become settled and decent citizens; for they cannot if they would, there is no opportunity. They would not if they could, for the desire is no longer existent.

We have already preventive detention for older persons, who, having been four times convicted of serious crime, are proved to be "habitual criminals." But hopeless as the older criminals are, the country is quite willing to adopt such measures and bear such expense as may be thought requisite for the purpose of detaining, and perchance reforming them.

But the young men for whom I now plead are a hundred times more numerous and a hundred times more hopeful than the old habitual criminals, whose position excites so much attention. We must have an oversea colony for these young men, and an Act of Parliament for the "preventive detention" of young offenders who are repeatedly convicted.

A third conviction should ensure every homeless offender the certainty of committal to the colony. This would stop for ever the senseless short imprisonment system, for we could keep them free of prison till their third conviction, when they should only be detained pending arrangement for their emigration.

The more I think upon this matter the more firmly I am convinced that nothing less will prevail. Though, of course, even with this plan, the young men who are hopelessly afflicted with disease or deformity must be excluded. For them the State must make provision at home, but not in prison.

A scheme of this character, if once put into active and thorough operation, would naturally work itself out, for year by year the number of young fellows to whom it would apply would grow less and less;

but while working itself out, it would also work out the salvation of many young men, and bring lasting benefits upon our country.

Vagrancy, with its attendant evils, would be greatly diminished, many prisons would be closed, workhouses and casual wards would be less necessary. The cost of the scheme would be more than repaid to the community by the savings effected in other ways. The moral effect also would be equally large, and the physical effects would be almost past computing, for it would do much to arrest the decay of the race that appears inseparable from our present conditions and procedure.

But the State must do something more than this; for many young habitual offenders are too young for emigration. For them the State reformatories must be established, regardless of their physical condition. To these reformatories magistrates must have the power of committal as certainly as they have the power of committal to prison. There must be no "by your leave," no calling in a doctor to examine the offender. But promptly and certainly when circumstances justify the committal to a State reformatory, the youthful offender should go. With the certainty that, be his physique and intellect what they may, he would be detained, corrected and trained for some useful life. Or, if found "quite unfit" or feeble-minded, sent to an institution suitable to his condition.

Older criminals, when proved to be mentally unsound, are detained in places other than prisons till their health warrants discharge. But the potential criminals among the young, no matter how often they are brought before the courts, are either sent back to hopeless liberty or thrust into prison for a brief period.

I repeat that philanthropy cannot attempt to deal with the habitual offenders, either in the days of their boyhood or in their early manhood. For philanthropy can at the most deal with but a few, and those few must be of the very best.

I cannot believe that our colonies would refuse to ratify the arrangement that I have outlined, if they were invited to do so by our own Government, and given proper security. They owe us something;

we called them into existence, we guarantee their safety, they receive our grit, blood and money; will they not receive, then, under proper conditions and safeguards, some of our surplus youth, even if it be weak? I believe they will!

In the strictures that I have ventured to pass upon the methods of the Salvation Army, I wish it to be distinctly understood that I make no attack upon the character and intentions of the men and women who compose it. I know that they are both earnest and sincere. For many of them I have a great admiration. My strictures refer to the methods and the methods only.

For long years I have been watchful of results, and I have been so placed in life that I have had plenty of opportunities for seeing and learning. My disappointment has been great, for I expected great things. Many other men and women whose judgment is entitled to respect believe as I do. But they remain silent, hoping that after all great good may come. But I must speak, for I believe the methods adopted are altogether unsound, and in reality tend to aggravate the evils they set out to cure. In 1900 I ventured to express the following opinion of shelters—

"EXTRACTS FROM 'PICTURES AND PROBLEMS'

"I look with something approaching dismay at the multiplication of these institutions throughout the length and breadth of our land. To the loafing vagrant class, a very large class, I know, but a class not worthy of much consideration, they are a boon. These men tramp from one town to another, and a week or two in each suits them admirably, till the warm weather and light nights arrive, and then they are off.

"This portion of the 'submerged' will always be submerged till some power takes hold of them and compels them to work out their own salvation.

"But there is such a procession of them that the labour homes, etc., get continual recruits, and the managers are enabled to contract for a great deal of unskilled work.

"In all our large towns there are numbers of self-respecting men, men who have committed no crime, save the unpardonable crime of growing old. Time was when such men could get odd clerical work, envelope and circular addressing, and a variety of light but irregular employment, at which, by economy and the help of their wives, they made a sort of living. But these men are now driven to the wall, for their poorly paid and irregular work is taken from them."

In 1911 A. M. Nicholl, in his not unfriendly book on GENERAL BOOTH AND THE SALVATION ARMY, makes the following statement, which I make no apology for reproducing.

His judgment, considering the position he held with the Army for so many years, is worthy of consideration. Here are some of his words—

"From an economic standpoint the social experiment of the Salvation Army stands condemned almost root and branch. So much the worse for economics, the average Salvation Army officer will reply. But at the end of twenty years the Army cannot point to one single cause of social distress that it has removed, or to one single act which it has promoted that has dealt a death-blow at one social evil....

"A more serious question, one which lies at the root of all indiscriminate charity, is the value to the community of these shelters. So far as the men in the shelters are benefited by them, they do not elevate them, either physically or morally. A proportion—what proportion?—are weeded out, entirely by the voluntary action of the men themselves, and given temporary work, carrying sandwich-boards, addressing envelopes, sorting paper, etc.; but the cause of their social dilapidation remains unaltered. They enter the shelter, pay their twopence or fourpence as the case may be (and few are allowed to enter unless they do), they listen to some moral advice once a week, with which they are surfeited inside and outside the shelter, they go to bed, and next morning leave the shelter to face the streets as they came in, The shelter gets no nearer to the cause of their depravity than it does to the economic cause of their failure, or to the economic remedy which the State must eventually introduce….

"The nomads of our civilisation wander past us in their fringy, dirty attire night by night. If a man stops us in the streets and tells us that he is starving, and we offer him a ticket to a labour home or a night shelter, he will tell you that the chances are one out of ten if he will procure admission. The better class of the submerged, or those who use the provision for the submerged in order to gratify their own selfishness, have taken possession of the vacancies, and so they wander on. If a man applies for temporary work, the choice of industry is disappointingly limited. One is tempted to think that the whole superstructure of cheap and free shelters has tended to the standardisation of a low order of existence in this netherworld that attracted the versatile philanthropist at the head of the Salvation Army twenty years ago….

"The general idea about the Salvation Army is, that the nearer it gets to the most abandoned classes, the more wonderful and the more numerous are the converts. It is a sad admission to pass on to the world that the opposite is really the case. The results are fewer. General Booth would almost break his heart if he knew the proportion of men who have been 'saved,' in the sense that he most values, through his social scheme. But he ought to know, and the Church and the world ought to know, and in order that it may I will make bold to say that the officials cannot put their hands on the names of a thousand men in all parts of the world who are to-day members of the Army who were converted at the penitent form of shelters and elevators, who are now earning a living outside the control of the Army's social work."

But the public appear to have infinite faith in the multiplication and enlargement of these shelters, as the following extract from a daily paper of December 1911 will show—

"'Since the days of Mahomet, not forgetting St. Francis and Martin Luther, I doubt if there is any man who has started, without help from the Government, such a world-wide movement as this.'

"This was Sir George Askwith's tribute to General Booth and the Salvation Army at the opening of the new wing of the men's Elevators in Spa Road, Bermondsey, yesterday afternoon. The task of declaring the wing open devolved upon the Duke of Argyll, who had beside him on the platform the Duchess of Marlborough, Lady St. Davids, Lord Armstrong, Sir Daniel and Lady Hamilton, Alderman Sir Charles C. Wakefield, Sir Edward Clarke, K.C., Sir George Askwith, and the Mayor of Bermondsey and General Booth.

"The General, who is just back from Denmark, spoke for three-quarters of an hour, notwithstanding his great age and his admission that he was 'far from well.' The Elevator, as its name implies, seeks to raise men who are wholly destitute and give them a fresh start. The new wing has been erected at a cost of L10,000, and the Elevator, which accommodates 590 men and covers two-and-a-half acres, represents an expenditure of L30,000, and is the largest institution of its kind in the world.

" 'The men,' said the General, 'are admitted on two conditions only, that they are willing to obey orders, and ready to work. Before he has his breakfast a man must earn it, and the same with each meal, the ticket given him entitling him to remuneration in proportion to the work he has done. If the men's conduct is good, they are passed on to another of the Army's institutions, and ultimately some post is secured for them through the employers of labour with whom the Army is in touch.' "

I believe General Booth to be sincere, and that he believes exactly what he stated. But even sincerity must not be allowed to mislead a generous public. Employers of labour do not, cannot, and will not keep positions open for General Booth or any other man. Employers require strong, healthy men who can give value for the wages paid. Thousands of men who have never entered shelters or prison are not only available but eager for positions that show any prospect of permanence, whether the work be heavy or skilled. For work that requires neither brains, skill or much physical strength, thousands of men whose characters are good are also available. I venture to say that General Booth cannot supply the public with a reasonable list of men who, having passed through the shelters, have been put into permanent work.

For every man and woman who is seeking to uplift their fellows I have heartfelt sympathy. For every organisation that is earnestly seeking to alleviate or remove social evils I wish abundant success. Against the organisations named I have not the slightest feeling. If they were successful in the work they undertake, no one in England would rejoice more than myself. But they are not successful, and because I believe that their claim to success blinds a well-intentioned and generous public, and prevents real consideration of deep-seated evils, I make these comments and give the above extracts.

I question whether any one in London knows better than myself the difficulty of finding employment for a man who is "down," for I have written hundreds of letters, I have visited numerous employers for this one purpose; I have begged and pleaded with employers, sometimes I have offered "security" for the honesty of men for whom I was concerned.

Occasionally, but only occasionally, was I successful. I have advertised on men's behalf frequently, but nothing worthy of the name of "work" has resulted. I know the mind of employers, and I know their difficulties; I have been too often in touch with them not to know. I have also been in touch with many men who have been in the shelters, elevators, bridges, labour homes and tents; I know their experience has been one of disappointment. I have written on behalf of such men to the "head-quarters," but nothing has resulted but a few days' work at wood-chopping, envelope addressing, or bill distributing, none of which can be called employment.

Day after day men who have been led to expect work wait, and wait in vain, in or about the head-quarters for the promised work that so rarely comes. For these men I am concerned, for them I am bold enough to risk the censure of good people, for I hold that it is not only cruel, but wicked to excite in homeless men hopes that cannot possibly be realised.

This point has been driven home to my very heart, for I have seen what comes to pass when the spark of hope is extinguished. Better, far better, that a man who is "down" should trust to his own exertions and rely upon himself than entertain illusions and rely upon others.

And now I close by presenting in catalogue form some of the steps that I believe to be necessary for dealing with the terrible problems of our great underworld.

First: the permanent detention and segregation of all who are classified as feeble-minded. Second: the permanent detention and segregation of all professional tramps. Third: proper provision for men and women who are hopelessly crippled or disabled. Fourth: establishment by the educational authorities, or by the State of reformatory schools, for youthful delinquents and juvenile adults regardless of physical weakness, deprivations or disease. Fifth: compulsory education, physical, mental and technical, up to sixteen years of age. Sixth: the establishment of municipal play-grounds and organised play for youths who have left school. Seventh: national and State-aided emigration to include the best of the "unfit." Eighth: the abolition of common lodging-houses, and the establishment of municipal lodging-houses for men and also for women. Ninth: the establishment of trade boards for all industries. Tenth: proper and systematic help for widows who have young children. Eleventh: thorough inspection and certification by local authorities of all houses and "dwellings" inhabited by the poor. Twelfth: housing for the very poor by municipal authorities, with abolition of fire-places, the heating to be provided from one central source. The housing to include a restaurant where nourishing but simple food may be obtained for payment that ensures a small profit. Thirteenth: more abundant and reasonable provision of work by the State, local authorities and for the unemployed. Fourteenth: a co-ordination of all philanthropic and charity agencies to form one great society with branches in every parish.

Give us these things, and surely they are not impossible, and half our present expensive difficulties would disappear. Fewer prisons, workhouses and hospitals would be required. The need for shelters and labour homes would not exist. The necessity for the activities of many charitable agencies whose constant appeals are so disturbing and puzzling, but whose work is now required, would pass away too.

But with all these things given, there would be still great need for the practice of kindness and the development of brotherly love. For without brotherly love and kindly human interest, laws are but cast-iron rules, and life but a living death. What is life worth? What can life be worth if it be only self-centred? To love is to live! to feel and take an interest in others is to be happy indeed, and to feel the pulses thrill.

And I am sure that love is abundant in our old country, but it is largely paralysed and mystified. For many objects that love would fain accomplish appear stupendous and hopeless. What a different old England we might have, if the various and hopeless classes that I have enumerated were permanently detained. For then love would come to its own, the real misfortunes of life would then form a passport to practical help. Widows would no longer be unceremoniously kicked into the underworld; accidents and disablements would no longer condemn men and women to live lives of beggary. Best of all, charitable and kindly deeds would no longer be done by proxy. It is because I see how professional and contented beggary monopolises so much effort and costs so much money; because I see how it deprives the really unfortunate and the suffering poor of the practical help that would to them be such a blessed boon, that I am anxious for its days to be ended. May that day soon come, for when it comes, there will be some chance of love and justice obtaining deliverance for the oppressed and deserving poor who abound in London's dark underworld.